W9-AEA-948

Public Finance and Public Choice

Two Contrasting Visions of the State

James M. Buchanan and
Richard A. Musgrave

The MIT Press
Cambridge, Massachusetts
London, England

Third printing, 2000

© 1999 Massachusetts Institute of Technology

This book was set in Palatino by Wellington Graphics.

Printed and bound in the United States of America.

Library of Congress Cataloging-in-Publication Data

Buchanan, James M.
  Public finance and public choice : two contrasting visions of the
  State / James M. Buchanan and Richard A. Musgrave.
    p.   cm.
  Includes bibliographical references and index.
  ISBN 0-262-02462-4 (alk. paper)
    1. Fiscal policy. 2. State, The. 3. Social choice.
I. Musgrave, Richard Abel, 1910– . II. Title.
HJ192.5.B83 1999
336.3—dc21   99-15446
                                                            CIP

Contents

Day 2

Day 3

Day 4

Day 5

Foreword

This book is a script of the papers and comments presented at a week of discussion between James Buchanan and Richard Musgrave that took place in the Freskensaal of the departments of Economics and Business at Munich's Ludwig-Maximilians University. The event was organized by the Center for Economic Studies. I am grateful to all participants and to those who provided technical aid, in particular Gertraud Porak, Carola Rottmann, Alex Popfinger, and the Bavarian TV. Financial Support by the Bayerische Rückversicherung and the Gesellschaft der Freunde der Universität is gratefully acknowledged. Special thanks are due to Valerie Morfill who typed the tape recordings and Jakob von Weizsäcker who served as copy editor. All material was checked and authorized by the respective authors and discussants. The video recordings of the seminar week are displayed on CES's Internet TV at http://www.ces.vwl.uni-muenchen.de.

Munich, November 1998
Hans-Werner Sinn

Day 1 (23 March 1998)

1.1 Introduction

Hans-Werner Sinn

Spectabiles, my dear guests and colleagues,

This promises to become the most interesting and important lecture series in the history of the Center for Economic Studies at the University of Munich. It is not unusual for the active participants of a conference to come from far away. However, it is unusual for the audience of a lecture series to do so, even though they are invited to participate actively in the discussions after the lectures. This shows just how famous our speakers must be.

James Buchanan and Richard Musgrave will present us with two contrasting visions of the state, in the hope that they will leave a legacy from which generations of economists will be able to profit.

Richard Musgrave is eighty-seven years old and James Buchanan is seventy-eight years. As you can imagine, it was not easy to convince them to come, but now they are here. We wish to applaud their energy and the dedication to the discipline of economics that they have proved by coming here.

Richard Musgrave and James Buchanan are both fathers of important fields of economics. Richard Musgrave laid the foundations of postwar public economics, and James Buchanan was the principal founder of the school of public choice. Both have influenced thousands of students and can count in hundreds the professional economists who are now following in their footsteps.

Both scholars have received countless honors and awards in the course of their lives. Most prominently, James Buchanan was awarded the Alfred Nobel Memorial Prize in Economic Sciences in 1986. He has also received eleven honorary doctorate degrees, nine after the Nobel prize and two before it. The two early degrees came from German-speaking universities. I welcome the representatives of the universities of Giessen and Zürich and congratulate them for their prescience. Richard Musgrave has "only" received five doctoral degrees. However, it is absolutely true when I say that Musgrave's degrees have all been awarded before his Nobel prize—a prize that is long overdue.

Richard Musgrave was born in 1910 in Königstein, Taunus, and he studied here in Munich at our department in 1930 and 1931. He attended lectures by, among others, Otto von Zwiedineck-Südenhorst and Adolf Weber. Unfortunately, he was too late to attend the lectures of Max Weber, who was also a member of our department, but Richard was able to read Max Weber's books, perhaps here in this room that is part of our library.

More important for Musgrave than Munich was the time he spent in Heidelberg where he enjoyed the renaissance of German public finance with Alfred Weber and Otto Pfleiderer, two important scholars of the time. I agree that the number of Webers in this story is confusing, but that is how it was. In Heidelberg, Musgrave received his Diploma in Economics (M.A.). I enjoy remembering the celebration at the fiftieth anniversary of that event in 1983, which I attended as a brand new university professor.

After finishing his studies, Musgrave then went to Rochester, not as yet a Jewish refugee, but a chosen scholar of the German Exchange Service. He did not return though. The terrible events in his motherland made it wise for him to stay where he was. He studied at Harvard and received his Ph.D. in 1937. In 1939, he published his seminal *Quarterly Journal of Economics* paper "Voluntary Exchange Theory of Public Finance," with which he laid the foundations for the theory of public goods that Paul Samuelson later converted from a positive to a normative theory. In these early years, he also published on budget problems and, together with Evsey Domar, on risk taking and taxation. The latter article is probably one of the most frequently cited articles in the history of economic thought.

Musgrave then worked for a number of years with the Federal Reserve System before he returned to academia in 1947. He taught at Swarthmore College, the University of Michigan, Johns Hopkins University, Princeton, and Harvard again from 1965 through to his retirement in 1981. He is still active now as adjunct professor in Santa Cruz.

Musgrave has written many books and about 150 articles in just about every field of public finance. Apart from his theory of public goods, what has most impressed me are his theory of deadweight losses, his work on international tax issues, his macroeconomic stabilization models, and his theory of fiscal federalism. His most important book is *The Theory of Public Finance*, which was published in 1959. This book has been a landmark in the field for decades, defining the issues and laying the foundations for the way public finance economists around the world think about the state.

The separation of government functions into the allocation, distribution and stabilization branches has turned out to be one of the most fruitful ideas in the history of the social sciences.

Musgrave has a social democratic background. He was influenced by the political ideas of the Weimar Republic, and he has grown out of the German public finance tradition. His thoughts can be traced back, and often developed in opposition, to public finance economists like Schäffle, Sax, and, in particular, Adolph Wagner, one of the Kathedersozialists and founders of the Verein für Socialpolitik—the German economic association. A consistently favorable view of the beneficial functions of the government sector has characterized Musgrave's work throughout his life.

Consistency is also the trait that characterizes James Buchanan. But Buchanan has been consistent in his suspicious views of the government. He has a liberal background and he is a genuine antiauthoritarian American, stemming from a renowned, though poor Tennessee family. As a boy, he went to the Buchanan school. The school received its name from Jim's grandfather, who had been the governor of Tennessee. Jim grew up on his family's farm, helping actively in its operation. I suspect that he became angry with the tax collectors whenever one of them dared to put his foot into Jim's territory.

James Buchanan describes his juvenile attitudes with the term "libertarian socialist." Note that this is nothing like the European variety of socialists. The libertarian socialist is exactly the opposite. He is antistate, antigovernment, and antiestablishment.

Buchanan's parents could not afford an expensive university education for their son. So they sent him to the State Teacher's College in Murfreesboro, Tennessee, where he graduated in 1940 with degrees in mathematics, English literature, and social sciences, which included economics. A year later, he also got his master of science in Tennessee. It was wartime, and so young Jim had to enroll in the Navy where he served in the Pacific area until the end of the war.

James Buchanan's true economic career began in Chicago where he received his Ph.D. in 1948 under Frank Knight. Knight converted the libertarian socialist into a libertarian market economist, one who was fascinated by the allocative achievements of the price mechanism.

In Chicago, James Buchanan also learned German and Italian, which helped him read the works of European scholars. But he was less impressed by the German tradition than by antiauthoritarian Italian writers and, in particular, by the Swedish economist Knut Wicksell. Wicksell's 1896 dissertation in German, *Finanztheoretische Untersuchungen*, fascinated him sufficiently to translate it later into the English language. There he found the principles of methodological individualism, homo oeconomicus, and politics-as-exchange that have characterized his work throughout his life. Interestingly enough, Richard Musgrave, too, sees his roots in Wicksell and Wicksell's student Lindahl. His 1939 paper on voluntary exchange relates to Wicksell as does his division of government activity into branches. He edited the book in which Buchanan's translation appeared. Wicksell is the bridge between our two scholars or better: the last common ancestor in the evolutionary tree of public-sector economics.

Buchanan taught at the University of Virginia, the University of California in Los Angeles, and the Virginia Polytechnic Institute. Since 1983, he has been at the Center for Study of Public Choice at George Mason University. He had opportunities, but was never tempted, to go to one of the famous East Coast universities, because he was afraid that he would be drawn into the mainstream of economic thought.

It is impossible to pay justice to Buchanan's academic achievements in this short introduction. However, a few words are appropriate. He modeled homo oeconomicus at the voting booth more convincingly than others, he taught us about the self-interest of politicians, he developed a theory of club goods, he warned us to include social constraints in the definition of Pareto optimality, and he made many important contributions to various other fields of economics and social sciences. In my view, his most important contribution is his book *The Calculus of Consent*, written jointly with Gordon Tullock. This book goes beyond the decision-making problem of the politician by analyzing political choices at the constitutional level. At the constitutional level, behind the veil of ignorance, it is easier to find the agreement between the economic agents that Wicksell had required for distributional policies. Chapter 13 of the book develops a path-breaking legitimation of redistributive policies that goes beyond Vickrey (Vickrey 1945), Friedman, Harsanhy, or Rawls. It comes up with surprisingly leftist conclusions and proves the scientific, nonideological nature of Buchanan's work.

My first personal contact with Buchanan's work was around 1970 in a seminar series with Herbert Timm in Münster, the German "public debt Pope," as he was called, which was devoted to the theme of Ricardian equivalence. I remember that Buchanan's paper on public debt was the most fascinating and difficult of all of the papers we discussed. We even communicated with him about his arguments. I was amused when I later saw Robert Barro's paper on public debt in 1974, because I had already known much of what

Barro said from the earlier work of James Buchanan and my present-day colleague Otto Gandenberger, who has also made important contributions to that issue.

Buchanan and Musgrave have often been misunderstood. A frequent contention is that Musgrave does normative public finance and Buchanan positive public finance. I wonder how the two of them see this. My impression is that they both use positive models of economic behavior with the ultimate goal of giving policy advice, and frankly I do not know why the taxpayer should pay for university professors if they are unable or unwilling to give such advice.

Musgrave typically uses positive models of private market behavior to derive Pareto improving rules for government intervention in the sense of ad hoc policies and even more so in the sense of designing tax and expenditure laws. In contrast, Buchanan concentrates on positive models of government intervention in this same sense in order to derive constitutional rules that constrain the ad hoc policies and the lawmaking procedure. Buchanan goes up a step in the hierarchy of political decision making, but there he is as normative as Musgrave is on the lower, interventionist level. Buchanan wants to show how the state *should* be organized and how governments *should* be constrained to make things better. Dennis Mueller (Mueller 1990) has recently made this point in an article on Buchanan's work. Of course, Buchanan's norm is always the benefit of the individual and not some abstract benefit of the state. But methodological individualism is the generally accepted concept of economics; it is not a dividing line between Buchanan's and Musgrave's normative views.

I believe that both public choice and public finance offer useful advice for public policy. Of course, we need good constitutional rules. But we also need good policies below that level of decision making. The two go hand in hand, and there are no contradictions.

Perhaps my point becomes clearer if a third level of economic decision making is introduced—namely, the decision making within a firm as studied by business economists. While the economist assumes that the firm maximizes profits, the business economist would lose his job if it really did. Contrary to first appearances, there is no contradiction between the economic and business administration views; they just represent two different levels of abstraction dictated by the need to find simplifications appropriate to the particular questions asked.

The public finance economist is the business economist of the state, and he is the constitutional economist of the business. Similarly the manager is a constitutional economist for his employees if he designs the incentive structure within his firm, and the public choice economist is the business economist of the constitutional assembly. In short, a hierarchy of human decision-making processes exists and the levels at which one applies normative or positive concepts depends on the problem to be studied. There is no such thing as a universally true level of abstraction.

This being said, it is time to begin the lectures.

1.2

Origins, Experiences,
and Ideas: A
Retrospective
Assessment

James M. Buchanan

I Introduction

I recall a line from Tennyson's poem, Ulysses: "I am a part
of all that I have met." The emphasis can be reversed by
stating "All that I have met is a part of me." Each one of us
exists within a set of parameters (the parameters of existence), which locate us in four-dimensional space-time. But
each of us brings to this state-of-being, this here and now, a
unique history that is unalterable by the fact that it has
happened. This history shapes our perceptions and our cog-
nition of that which we observe, interpret, and evaluate.

Each person, as a separately existent unit of consciousness, looks at, hears, feels, and tastes that which is confronted through a "different window," to use Nietzsche's
wonderful metaphor. Each person "constructs" reality from
the elements at hand and somehow integrates the natural
and artifactual parameters of existence into an interpretation
and understanding that defines human being. Acceptance of
this proposition does not, however, imply that reality itself
exists only as constructed separately by persons; we need
not embrace extreme solipsism. Again, Nietzsche's metaphor rescues us. We do look at the world through differing

windows, but we are, after all, looking at the same world. Reality is not wholly imaginary; we do indeed stub our toe when we kick a rock.

Social reality is not basically different from physical reality in its existence independent of human imagination. But the ultimate object of observation in social reality is human behavior, and the presumption of volition on the part of actors creates a potential for differences in interpretation and understanding that is absent from any inquiry into harder stuff. The brick that topples from the wall could not have chosen not to fall. Observers (scientists) can readily reach shared understandings as to why that event occurred, even if separate observers might have seen the event from a different perspective. Compare the brick with the person who is observed to take the left rather than the right fork in the road as traveled. Explanation—understanding of the action that is observed—becomes difficult because of the presumption that choice was possible; the actor was not hard-wired, as if genetically, to take that action that was observed to be taken.

The social philosophers-scientists of the eighteenth century advanced our understanding at this point by their discovery that general uniformities in human nature do exist that allow falsifiable predictions to be made concerning the patterns of behavioral responses to changes in constraints, even if each single actor is presumed able to choose voluntarily among the options that are confronted. From this basic discovery, the science of economics emerged, articulated in Adam Smith's great treatise, *The Wealth of Nations* (1776).

The explanatory limits of this science must, however, be recognized. Consider the central hypothesis: As the relative price of a marketed good falls, a larger quantity will be voluntarily purchased. Note precisely what is being claimed by this hypothesis. There is no implication that each and every prospective purchaser must increase the quantity purchased. Each person remains free to choose. The hypothesis of demand states only that, for the whole set of prospective purchasers, a larger quantity will be taken than before the relative price reduction. Further, and by the same logic, there is nothing in the law of demand that allows any prediction as to how much the increase in quantity will be. (There is no uniformity in elasticities implied by the law of demand.)

I shall not go further into methodological detail. The discussion should be sufficient to suggest that different observers, each one of whom fully operates within the basic research program of economic science, may differ widely in their ultimate understanding and interpretation of the social reality that the political economy reflects. Each observer may meet all standards for qualification as an economic scientist, yet each may retain a uniquely personal understanding-interpretation of the phenomena under inquiry, as determined in part by historical experience.

The problem of attaining scientific consensus among those who consider socioeconomic-political reality is further exacerbated by the relative importance in extending the inquiry into "other worlds" than that which is known to be existent. For the physical scientist, the overwhelming proportion of the task lies in explaining the reality as it is, with very little attention paid to alternative structures. For the social scientist, by contrast, because of the underlying presupposition that social reality is itself artifactual rather than natural, the motivating force behind much effort lies in the prospect that this reality may be reconstructed or reformed so as to make for a "better" world. Accordingly, more analysis must be placed on examination of that which might be as opposed to that which is, with the necessary implication that differences in interpretation are wider in the first than in the second of these stages of inquiry.

I have gone through this preliminary discussion, which we might call notes on the philosophy of science, in order to explain why Professor Musgrave and I, in our planning session for this symposium, chose to commence with separate lectures in which each of us will identify formative influences that have affected our separate visions or perspectives on the political economy of the modern society. My point of emphasis here is that both of us remain practicing economist scientists, in the proper meaning of this term, despite the fact that our visions of socioeconomic-political reality remain substantially different. Also, and this is important, I note that neither of us approaches the subject matter ideologically, in the ordinary meaning of this term. Neither of us starts from some preconceived political-philosophical stance, and neither of us has been associated closely with this or that political party, movement, or cult.

Why, then, do our separate visions differ? To offer a partial answer, we propose, in these introductory lectures, to isolate and to identify what we now think to have been determining factors, involving origins, persons, experiences, and ideas, each as now assigned our own retrospective weighting.

II Origins

I shall not go into autobiographical detail (for extended discussion see my set of autobiographical essays, *Better Than Plowing*, 1992). However, some narrative is necessary to identify the early influences that now seem to me to have been important in shaping my ultimate vision.

By heritage, I am Scots-Irish. All of my known ancestors were progeny of the mid–eighteenth-century wave of

American immigrants from Northern Ireland, who were themselves transplanted from Scotland a century earlier. Much of the whole southeastern United States was initially settled by these hardy Scots-Irish, who were solidly Presbyterian and fiercely independent.

I was born and reared in the upper South of the country, in middle Tennessee, a region that was Confederate in loyalties during the great Civil War of the 1860s, but which had never been a plantation society, as such. That war itself cannot be overlooked as a formative influence. In a genuine sense, I grew up as a member of a defeated people in a war that was still remembered by my grandparents. From this fact of history alone, any strongly held pronationalist sentiment, if translated into unquestioning loyalty or fealty to federal or central government authority, would have been near-treachery. At the very least, there could have been, for me, no sense of membership in a genuine national community. Hegelian actualization in the United States would have remained beyond my consciousness, regardless of the career path chosen.

Apart from the generalized Southern attitude toward the authority of the central nation-state, my own family's history was important. My paternal grandfather was elected governor of Tennessee, the highest elected state office, in the populist uprising of the early 1890s. The populists defined themselves through their opposition to the Eastern establishment, the robber barons and financial tycoons, who were also alleged to control national politics. Much of my early reading was found, literally, in pile upon pile of pamphlet literature of the 1890s. It is no surprise to me that I have always been sympathetic to the emotional appeal exerted by those who advance grand conspiracy theories. This set of attitudes was reinforced by personal experience in military

training for World War II during which I personally felt
myself a victim of anti-southern discrimination.

III From the Academy

Only after World War II did I become an academic economist
in any meaningful sense. And I entered graduate school at
the University of Chicago in January 1946 as a committed
"libertarian socialist." (These terms may seem contradictory,
although there was a political party in Weimar Germany that
used this label.) I was libertarian in my conviction that
politicized restrictions on individual liberties should be
minimized. But I was socialist in my judgment that only
political action could break up and control the power con-
centrations that directed economic life.

In retrospect, I now realize that, quite simply, I remained
illiterate in my understanding of the coordinating properties
of markets. It is not at all surprising, therefore, that I was
intellectually receptive to such an understanding, once it
was offered to me by an articulate spokesman, a role filled
for me by Professor Frank Knight, who quickly became my
role model. It is because Knight himself was not an ide-
ologue—indeed, he had written one of the most penetrating
criticisms of capitalist economic organization (Knight
1935)—that his teaching proved so persuasive to me. And
again, it is not at all surprising, when viewed in retrospect,
that, once I fully understood the principle of spontaneous
coordination effected through the workings of markets, the
libertarian socialist should become the libertarian advocate
of laissez-faire within limits. (I entitled the chapter in my
autobiographical essays relating these experiences "Born
Again Economist.")

One characteristic feature of graduate training in Chicago,
then as well as now, warrants mentions here. The Chicago

economist does not project an image of becoming an adviser to governments, thereby proffering advice on how to manage national economies, in the large or in the small. The Chicago economist learns how economies work rather than how economies might be controlled. Of course, this generalization has its notable exceptions, but the contrast in professional attitudes in this respect between Chicago and, say, Harvard, may be critical in influencing both career and research paths.

IV Public Finance, Politics, and Knut Wicksell

My specialization within economies was, by prior interest, public finance, and my acquired understanding of and appreciation for the functioning of markets offered little or no assistance toward any understanding of the workings of the public economy. Very early in my graduate study, I was struck by the naivete of the textbook commonplaces about political reality, at least as evidenced in the English-language versions. It seemed self-evident to me that some model of politics is necessary before any analysis, positive or normative, of taxing and public spending could proceed. At about this time, I discovered the English translation of de Viti de Marco's *First Principles of Public Finance* (de Viti 1936), which stimulated my interest in looking further into the Italian sources. One of my first papers, which I called "The Pure Theory of Public Finance" (Buchanan 1949), was nothing more than a plea to my fellow economists to be more explicit about their political presuppositions.

These early attitudes reflected my unwillingness to acquiesce in the conventional presumption that the state, or collectivity, was everywhere benevolent, or, at least, that it may be presumed to be so for the purpose of analytical exercise. Note that, in this early inquiry, I was never attracted by the

quasi-anarchist libertarian stance that rejects the potential
efficacy of any and all collective action. I accepted the necessary politicization of the framework within which the
market economy must operate, and I also recognized the
potential efficiency in collective provision and financing of
commonly shared goods and services. But how is it possible
for persons to organize themselves collectively or politically
so as to secure the genuine benefits from collective action
without, at the same time, leaving open the prospects for
exploitation?

It was precisely in confrontation with this age-old question in political philosophy that my personal discovery of
Knut Wicksell's *Finanztheoretische Untersuchungen* (Wicksell
1896) was so important. Wicksell's efforts seem to match
closely with my own, since he seemed to be searching for
some practical resolution to the basic question. Wicksell
found it necessary to examine the institutional structure
through which collective decisions are made, and to pay
heed specifically to the rules. He recognized explicitly that
only by changes in rules could changes in patterns of
outcomes be predicted to emerge. In passing, Wicksell
sharply criticized his fellow economists for their unchal-
lenged presumption that government is best modeled as a
benevolent despot, simply waiting for the economists' advice. Wicksell's dissertation was indeed music to my mind,
and surely he deserves pride of place among the several
influences that have shaped my basic ideas on the political
economy.

V Arrow's Impossibility Theorem and Italian Realism

I have now described where my ideas were, more or less,
at mid-century. But early in the 1950s these ideas were

reinforced by my reactions to the academic discussions aroused by Kenneth Arrow's 1951 book, *Social Choice and Individual Values*. Both Arrow himself and his many critics seemed disturbed by the implications of his impossibility theorem. They seemed, somehow, to place positive value on the existence of some internally consistent and coherent "public interest" or "social welfare," quite independent of any relationship to the preferences of individuals who are members of the community. My 1954 criticism (Buchanan 1954) of the whole discussion called into question the meaningfulness of any such construction as a "social welfare function," and it specifically contrasted the emergent properties of markets with those reflected in explicit collective choices, as made within defined rules.

In my early forays into analyses of collective action, however, my attitudes retained residues of a romantic vision of both politics and politicians. Despite the intellectual stimulation offered by Wicksell's insights, I remained stubbornly defensive of the political institutions of "democracy," without any real willingness to subject such institutions to analytical challenge. The Italian year (1955–1956) was a necessary element in finally sweeping away the romantic cobwebs about democratic processes. I mentioned earlier that my initial interest in the Italian scholars was provoked by their general recognition of the necessary relationship between the public economy and political structure. I spent the full academic year exploring the classic Italian works in "scienze della finanze," with special attention to the modeling of politics. I came away with a healthy dose of Italian realism about politicians, politics, and bureaucracy. The whole Italian culture incorporates attitudes toward governance that could, indeed, "shock" the American sensibilities, as formed before mid-century.

VI *The Calculus of Consent*

Frank Knight's emphasis on the structural features of economic order (Knight 1933), Knut Wicksell's demonstration
that collective decision rules can be adjusted to yield generally preferred outcomes without exploitation along with his
criticism of economists' implicit models of governments, the
realistic inquiry of the Italians into the motivations of politicians—these elements mixed with my own libertarian sym-
pathies, my rejection of economists' romantic blinders about
politics, including my reaction to the discussion surrounding Arrow's theorem—combined to create, for me, a setting
for research and inquiry that was ripe for further development. But a catalyst was needed, and this was provided by
a prospective coauthor, Gordon Tullock, who brought to the
enterprise a hard-nosed emphasis on the predictive and
explanatory power of *Homo economicus* models in politics
and bureaucracy. This emphasis was evoked by Tullock's
years in the foreign service. Having been influenced by the
economics of Henry Simons and Ludwig von Mises, as
supplemented by the precursory public choice insights of
Joseph Schumpeter and Anthony Downs, Tullock was critical for me both as a means of bolstering my confidence in
mounting a challenge to much of the conventional wisdom
in political science and as a source of genuinely creative and
original ideas, due, in some part at least, to the fact that he
had never been personally exposed to the little orthodoxies
of mid-century social sciences.

We launched the project that became *The Calculus of Consent* (Buchanan and Tullock 1962) without any internal anticipation that we were writing a book that might ultimately
be judged seminal. We were, much more simply understood,
using the tools and methods of the economic analysis and

concepts available at the time in application to the constitutional organization of a polity. And, in so doing we were effectively, translating some of the philosophical ideas of James Madison and the other founding fathers, ideas that had, been embedded in the American documents. We thought of our effort as aimed at providing at least an analytical framework within which the operation of United States politics, both as observed and imagined, might be modeled and, finally, understood, a necessary step before constructive reform might be attempted. By the nature of the enterprise, our analysis was reductionist and general, but we made no effort to conceal the essential American provinciality of any application.

In a comprehensive overview, *The Calculus of Consent* may be interpreted as an intellectual attack on majoritarianism and majority rule, since we removed these institutions from the sacrosanct status implicitly assigned to them in much of the prevailing orthodoxy. By inference, therefore, our book might have been taken to be a criticism of parliamentary systems of governance, which elevate majority rule to dominance, along with a defense of republican systems in which majorities are constrained. More specifically, the normative thrust of our inquiry offered support for constitutional limits on the exercise of political authority.

VII The 1960s, Anarchy, and Leviathan

Viewed from the end-of-century perspective, *The Calculus of Consent* was analytically optimistic in the sense that the argument laid out a structural basis both for understanding the American sociopolitical order and for prospects of making this order work more effectively. But it is now also important to recognize that *The Calculus of Consent* was

completed before the 1960s happened. And, as that tumultuous decade played itself out, my own attitudes toward
both the vulnerability and viability of the American socioeconomic-political order were dramatically modified. We
could not have written *The Calculus of Consent* in 1972, a
decade after its initial date of publication.

Too much had changed. I personally observed and sensed
that the established order was crumbling; the academies of
the land allowed decades of steady, if erratic, progress to be
swept away almost without resistance. Methods, manners,
morals, and standards were cavalierly tossed on the junk
heap of history. In politics, governments everywhere, socialist and nonsocialist, overreached themselves and demon-
strably failed to deliver what they had promised. In the
United States, nonelected members of a judicial elite took
on authority that was acknowledged to be legislative.

My own take on all of this was that we seemed, simultaneously and along separate dimensions, to be plunging into
anarchistic chaos and into uncheckable exploitation under
the weight of a Leviathan government. Democracy seemed
unable to control its own excesses, and any semblance of
constitutional understanding seemed to have suddenly
disappeared.

This setting prompted me to shift my attention to more
basic questions than those that had occupied my interest as
a political economist. Somehow I sensed the need to examine, at least to my own satisfaction, the fundamental issues
of political legitimacy. How is politically organized coercion
of individuals ever justified? What are the boundaries of
collective action? I found myself becoming a political phi-
losopher, in inquiry if not by profession. And out of this
emerged, finally, the book *The Limits of Liberty* (1975a). The
subtitle of this book was "Between Anarchy and Leviathan,"

which is descriptive of my search for some institutional means of achieving and maintaining some appropriate structure of political order in balance—a structure that handles the continuing tension between the opposing pulls, between too little and too much politicization, too little and too much collective intrusion into the liberties of citizens, too small and too large relative sizes of the public economy.

Having made my best effort to articulate my own understanding of philosophical foundations in *The Limits of Liberty*, it seemed evident to me that prospects for any reform or improvement must lie in the design and construction of effective constitutional constraints on governance. The apparent failures of democratic regimes to adhere to ordinary principles for fiscal prudence seemed to be the most obvious illustration of irresponsibility. My judgment, then and now, is that this period of fiscal irresponsibility was to be explained by the sometime dominance of Keynesian nostrums, an argument that was spelled out in the book *Democracy in Deficit* (Buchanan and Wagner 1977), written jointly with Richard Wagner. The normative inference from the argument involved support for a constitutional amendment of budget balance in the United States.

More comprehensively, there seemed to be a need to analyze the fiscal constitution in toto. To do this, a model of government is required even if, at one level of analysis, it is recognized that government is itself a complex interaction process with no internally coherent choice function. In research initiated jointly with Geoffrey Brennan, we found that a model embodying revenue maximization offered interesting insights. We first formulated and then tried analytically to answer the question: If government, as it actually operates, tends to maximize revenues from any and every source assigned under constitutional authority, how should these sources be limited? Behind an appropriately drawn Rawlsian veil, how much fiscal authority would be constitutionally allowed to be exercised through ordinary politics?

The analysis of these questions, presented in our book *The Power to Tax* (Brennan and Buchanan 1980), carried normative implications that tended to challenge much of the conventional wisdom. The revenue-maximizing government offered a specific alternative to the benevolent government presumed in orthodox treatments, with categorically different implications for the structure of tax policy. Our argument was severely criticized by several economists, including Richard Musgrave. Central to the objection was our presumed elevation of the Leviathan or revenue-maximizing model of government to an implied descriptive role.

Brennan and I considered this objection to be grounded on a misunderstanding of our whole enterprise, which was basically precautionary rather than positive. We were, in this respect, following Max Weber in setting up one of many ideal types of political structure, each one of which may yield its own separate set of insights into the complex politics that may actually be observed. The centrality and seriousness of the criticisms, however, stimulated us to follow up *The Power to Tax* with a second book, *The Reason of Rules* (1985), in which we shifted attention away from the fiscal constitution and addressed the whole set of issues summarized in our subtitle "Constitutional Political Economy." I shall discuss many of the issues in my second lecture (Day 3).

VIII The Economics of Ethics

In the period after 1985, my interests have proceeded in two different, but ultimately related, directions, only one of which might seem to fall strictly within the general constitutional analysis. The first of these research programs has long been included in my inclusive portfolio of ideas, a program that involves the intersection between ethics and economics, again perhaps owing to the early influence of Frank Knight. I have argued, over the course of decades, that formal constraints on behavior, as laid down in legal and constitutional structures, can never alone be sufficient to insure viability in social order. An underlying set of ethical norms or standards seems essential, although we recognize that formal and informal constraints become substitutes at some margins of adjustment.

How can the economic effect of ethical constraints be analyzed? For me, a strong intuitive sense that the presence of a work ethic must exert positive effects on economic well-being could not readily be incorporated in the corpus of orthodox neoclassical economic theory. Puzzlement at this juncture made me call into question my own long-undisturbed acceptance of the neoclassical postulates. Only when I came to realize that the presumption of economy-wide constant returns acts to remove all ethical content from the work-leisure choice margin did I rediscover the increasing-returns strand of inquiry, extending from Adam Smith, through Allyn Young, and Nicolas Kaldor, and into modern theories of trade and endogenous growth, as represented by Paul R. Krugman, Wilfred J. Ethier, Paul M. Romer, Xiao Kai Yang, and others. With my colleague, Yong J. Yoon, I found myself plunged directly into basic economic theory for the first time in decades, and particularly in tracing the implications of generalized increasing returns (Buchanan and Yoon 1994). Only in such an analytical construction can the economic impact of ethical constraints on personal behavior be fully understood. Clearly, generalized increasing returns carries some implications for the evaluation of the relative efficacy of market and collective allocation of resources, but these implications remain as yet unexplored terrain on my research agenda.

IX The Generality Principle in Politics

The second research program that has occupied my energies during the late 1980s and early 1990s is somewhat more consistent with my continuing interests in constitutional limits on political action. As noted earlier, *The Calculus of Consent* was influenced primarily by Wicksell, and the avenues for constitutional reform that were stressed in that book involved modifying majoritarian processes toward more inclusion, at least for critically important collective actions. Over the three decades after that early book was published, I came increasingly, if reluctantly, to the realization or judgment that majoritarian institutions are so closely related in public attitudes to "democracy" that reform efforts aimed toward more inclusive decision rules would probably fail. In other words, if additional constitutional limits are desired, alternative means must be found that do not seem to undermine majoritarianism.

This motivation led me to concentrate attention on possible changes in the permissible set of outcomes available for majority choice, an approach that had been presaged in *The Power to Tax*, with respect to tax institutions in particular. At this point in my inquiry, I returned to Hayek's treatise, *The Constitution of Liberty* (F. A. Hayek 1960), which offered an eloquent argument to the effect that the rule of law, interpreted as the principle of generality, is a necessary feature of any free society. It was then relatively simple to marry the Hayekian ideas with my own long-held emphases on the need for constitutional limits on ordinary democratic politics. If majorities can be restricted to the enactment of laws, including those that involve taxing and spending, that apply generally—that is, nondiscriminatorily—over all classes and groups in the political community, the worst excesses of modern distributional politics (de Jasay's "churning state" [de Jasay 1985]) might be avoided. The basic analysis here, along with applications, is developed in some detail in a book written jointly with Roger Congleton and titled *Politics by Principle, Not Interest: Toward Nondiscriminatory Democracy* (Buchanan and Congleton 1998).

The normative thrust of the argument does indeed depart from my earlier advocacy of Wicksellian reforms aimed at supramajority rules in legislative assemblies. I have not, of course, abandoned the acceptance of the Wicksellian efficiency logic. But a recognition that Wicksellian reforms may be impossible to attain prompts my currently held judgment that the "political efficiency" generated by an operative generality constraint may more than offset any "economic efficiency" gains that might be promised, but never gained, by Wicksellian projections.

X Conclusions

What I have tried to do in this introductory lecture is to offer my own version of an intellectual odyssey over the course of more than a half century. I hope that it makes for a somewhat informed understanding of my own window on the political economy. As we recognize, of course, any view "from the inside looking out" is likely to be quite different from those "from the outside looking in." And even a personalized inside assessment is transient, as my narrative suggests.

Perhaps I can best end the lecture by combining the metaphors of Nietzsche and Heraclitus. I have traced some of the elements that may have shaped my window on the reality of political economy. But my window tomorrow, in 2000, will not offer the same vision as today, and for both of the familiar reasons. My own perceptions, understandings, and interpretations must change through time. And that which is observed must be ever-changing.

1.3

The Nature of the Fiscal State: The Roots of My Thinking

Richard A. Musgrave

I Introduction

My assignment in this first lecture is to examine the roots of my thinking on the role of the state and its fiscal role in particular. These roots draw on a rich and diverse body of thought, ancient as well as contemporary, with some of it entering my own vision and some helpful in clarifying what to reject. Sampling that list, one finds Locke as well as Bentham; Sidgwick as well as Harsanyi and Rawls; Smith as well as Wagner; Wicksell and Lindahl as well as Pigou and Samuelson; Downs as well as Buchanan and Tullock; Marx as well as Weber; Schanz and Simons as well as Edgeworth and Mirrlees; Schumpeter as well as Keynes and Hansen, and so forth. As this list suggests, my fascination with the field has been rooted in its broad scope, a joining of economics, politics and social ethics. As building blocks in the vision of a good society, these names encompass the two traditions in my intellectual and academic background, beginning here in Munich (1930) and Heidelberg (1931–1932), followed by emigration to the United States in 1933 and graduate studies at Harvard (1934–1937). Both settings shaped my own view of society and its public sector, leaving me anchored at, say, 50 degrees longitude, west of the mid-Atlantic. Looking back, I think that mixed intellectual ancestry proved a net gain but also tended to make mine a somewhat special case. I have described this elsewhere (R. A. Musgrave 1997a) and need not recount it here.

Books and ideas aside, there were also the tumultuous events that passed by—World War I, the Russian Revolution, German inflation, reparations, Hitler's rise, the Great Depression, *Kristallnacht*, World War II, the fall of communism, the renaissance of the market, Vietnam, and, especially in the United States, a shift away from faith in the public sector to skepticism if not hostility toward it. Hardly a model of harmony and equilibrium, my century saw the autocratic state at its worst, but it also traced a path toward a democratic and social-minded society. I shared that vision early on when the hopes of the Weimar Republic offered a first if fleeting glimpse of what might have been, and then again in the buoyant atmosphere of the New Deal years and the earlier 1960s. Mistakes made and inevitable correction notwithstanding, the trend was toward a democratic society and I do not regret having shared it.

II Clearing the Way

Before turning to the key functions of the fiscal state and their principles of operation, a few comments on the nature of that state and the methodology of fiscal economics are in order. This is appropriate especially since our discourse is to offer two views of the state and its fiscal order.

Nature of the Fiscal State

Fiscal resources are needed to execute state functions, and the way in which they are rendered shapes how individuals and the state are related. The role of the state is not that of the mercantilist court designed to protect and enrich the prince, who may draw on his subjects as part of his domain. Nor is the state to be seen as an organic unit wherein the individual is absorbed in the "whole," or as a benevolent dictator who knows and meets the wishes of his subjects. Instead, I think of the state as an association of individuals, engaged in a cooperative venture, formed to resolve problems of social coexistence and to do so in a democratic and fair fashion. The state, in short, is a contractarian venture, based on and reflecting the shared concerns of its individual members.

The state and its public sector thus form an integral part of a multifaceted socioeconomic order. The wishes and concerns of individuals are what matters, but their appropriate modes of interaction differ with the nature of their separate and mutual concerns. In a world of private goods, the market and individual exchange offer the efficient mode, but this is only part of the problem. Social coexistence also involves externalities that are not met by the market but instead require a political process—call it the state—for efficient resolution. Public policy enters, not as an aberration from the "natural order" of private markets but as an equally valid or natural means of addressing a different set of problems. The visible hand of budgetary processes, in short, is no less "natural" than the invisible hand of the market. A variety of needs are to be met and tasks to be undertaken, some better served by the former and others by the latter mode. Failures arise and need to be dealt with under both, with both rendering essential and complementary contributions to the social order.

That order, I hasten to add, includes not only the Pareto efficient use of resources, important though that is, but also other and no less vital dimensions of social coexistence—

distributive justice and the balance of individual rights and obligations upon which a meaningful concept of liberty has to be built. A view of fiscal economics, which holds that all is well if only Pareto optimality prevails, bypasses these essential components of social coexistence and fails on both normative and positive grounds. Without allowing for a sense of social justice the good society cannot be defined, and without it democratic society cannot function.

Individuals, Groups, and Community

The state, as a cooperative venture among individuals, must reflect their interests and concerns. Its foundation in that basic sense has to be individualistic. At the same time, individuals do not live in isolation but are members of a group and thereby have common concerns. Social choices, though individually based are conditioned by group association. Efficient provision of public goods requires political institutions and a collective process of policy determination. In a democratic society, consensus is required and the individual voter functions in the context of group choice. Coalitions are part of that process. Marx had it right when viewing social interaction in terms of group interests, even though he was mistaken in placing exclusive weight on a simple labor-capital dichotomy. Many other shared concerns, economic and otherwise also arise and intersect each other. Schumpeter (Schumpeter 1942) was similarly correct when viewing the course of social development as driven by changing patterns of social structure, as was Weber in introducing the role of shared values as a determining factor. Decision making in fiscal economics, therefore, should be seen in this broader context of social structure and not in simple analogy to individuals, engaged in maximizing their self-interests in the market.

Individuals, in the last resort, are the acting agents, and not the state or groups "as such," but it does not follow that they may not also value membership in their community and the sharing of common concerns. Overrepresented in my German and underrepresented in my U.S. years, I am well aware that the concept of community is open to abuse—how could I not be, after having experienced the disruptions of lectures here in Munich and book burnings in Heidelberg before leaving Germany in 1933? At the same time, the concept of community should not be exorcised for that reason. Self-interest is not all that matters, nor can the good society be based on it alone. Liberty, as I see it, is not to be defined as absence of restraint and self- centered interest only. Rather, a meaningful concept of liberty calls for limitations imposed by mutual concern for others. "To individuality," as Mill put it, "belongs that part of life in which it is chiefly the individual that is interested; to society, the part which chiefly interests society" (Mill 1859, 92).

State Institutions

The state as a cooperative undertaking derives its authority from its individual members, who are the ultimate agents. Nevertheless, the state in expediting that cooperation needs an institutional form, and it is in this qualified sense that the state "as such" may be said to exist. As any operating institution, the state requires delegation of authority and subfunctions. Depending on the particular constitutional form (e.g., the parliamentary systems of Europe or the executive system of the United States), these functions will be structured in various ways, including executive, legislative and judiciary functions, each supported by bureaus rendering professional and administrative services.

It is especially at the level of bureaucracy where the cameralist image of *Finanzwissenschaft* as a how-to-do handbook for civil servants enters. That image of an efficient and well-functioning fiscal bureau retained its reach into the high period of German public finance in the closing decades of the nineteenth century. Gerhard Colm's view of the service agency (Colm 1927) still reflected that image, as did his conduct of the U.S. Bureau of the Budget during the 1940s. Two decades later, that spirit again blossomed in the emergence of cost-benefit analysis. It is here that the contribution of bureaucracy or, to use my preferred term, civil service, is most vital.

Apart from finding efficient solutions to reaching set targets, there is also the need for substantive leadership in the selection of policy goals. This involves not only correct transmission of voter preferences via elected representatives but also political leadership on their part and at the executive level of government. Such leadership, at both the parliamentary and executive levels of government, undertaken at the risk of censure by the voting public, adds a further and essential input into a functioning system of democratic government, including in particular its fiscal operations.

That vision of efficient government, to be sure, is not a carbon copy of what occurs but a standard by which performance can be measured, similar to corresponding standards by which efficient performance of households and firms in the private sector are assessed. Actual performance will differ among governments and periods of time, but efficient conduct and constructive leadership are not beyond reach. I need only recall Roosevelt's role in the early 1930s and Churchill's at the outset of World War II. Nor is it beyond the capacity of representatives and officials to seek the public interest, even where this may put reelection into question. The citizen needs protection against abusive government when his or her rights are infringed, but modeling government on the presumption of lazy bureaucrats and self- aggrandizing or corrupt officials (Niskanen 1971; Brennan and Buchanan 1980) offers a biased picture. Its propagation has been destructive of good government in a democratic society.

III Methodology

It remains to note two points of methodology, both traced to Max Weber's towering figure in my early years. First, there is his concept of "ideal type" as a rational and consistent set of actions directed at achieving a normative goal. While the actual performance of agents and of social institutions, be they market or public sector, follow a mixed pattern, it is nevertheless fruitful to define a normative goal and to model how actions *should* be shaped so as to meet it. Just as homo economicus or a competitive Walrasian system are useful fictions to model an ideal market, so it is helpful to visualize how a correctly functioning public sector would perform. While the resulting vision of the well-behaved public sector (or market) remains a normative abstraction, it is needed nevertheless. Unless "correct" solutions are established to serve as standards, defects and failures of actual performance cannot even be identified. Pragmatism, standing by itself, is meaningless as a guide to public policy. Whether for the market or the public sector, the vision of a first-best solution is needed to identify a feasible second-best. It is in that sense that my concern has been with "good" government and "good" expenditure or tax systems and will be viewed as such in my papers for this symposium.

Next, there is Weber's distinction between "value relevance" and "value judgment." The proposition is that one can investigate and establish causal relationships between value-relevant factors and outcomes—for example, the bearing of puritan ethics on the rate of saving, or the efficiency costs of egalitarian policies—and that this can (and should) be done without permitting the analyst's own valuation of outcomes to affect his findings. Scientific analysis, as Weber argued, should aim to be value-free; and contrary to the current deconstructionist fashion I share that view, old-fashioned though this may be.

At the same time, valuation of outcomes enters and especially so in fiscal economics. Compatible with Weber's dictum, a distinction may be drawn between the role of ideology in choosing what is to be researched and in doing the research. A researcher may properly permit his values to enter when choosing the hypothesis to be tested and be pleased or displeased with the outcome, while obliged to be objective when conducting the analysis. But this is no simple task. What at first sight may seem purely technical questions (e.g., the elasticities of saving or labor supply) soon assume policy implications and carry ideological weights in supporting or questioning alternative visions of what makes a good society. Formulating the problem (i.e., choosing the variables that are to be included or econometric techniques to be used) may itself become a strategy for reaching hoped-for results. Competition for winning the case with the profession as jury then becomes a wholesome process.

IV Allocation and the Provision of Public Goods

I now leave these broader concerns raised by the nature of the fiscal state and turn to its key tasks. You will not be surprised if I do this by returning to my three branches as I defined them now four decades ago (R. A. Musgrave 1959). I still find them a useful framework, not only for expository textbook purposes that they have served well but also as an analytical device to distinguish between the key issues, that is, the nature of public goods and why they need be provided for, the place of equity and distributive justice in the design of fiscal systems and the role of budgets in the macro performance of the economy. While any one program—for example, a highway project and its finance or a tax reform—may bear on all three issues, their underlying logic nevertheless differs. This first paper is to show where I come from in each of these spheres, leaving their application to specific policy issues for later rounds.

First to be considered is the provision of public goods. Provision, as I use the term, means the political process by which such goods are made available, and *not* their public production. The issue of public ownership of the means of production, the key feature of socialism, is only peripheral to my fiscal economics. The institution of the public sector is needed to complement, not replace, the private sector and has nothing to do with socialism as an alternative order. It should hardly be necessary to make that point but it is, especially so since the seminal paper on optimal taxation (Diamond and Mirrlees 1972) was misleadingly entitled "Optimal Taxation and Public Production."

Beginnings

The theory of public goods is no novel concern. Hume, two and a half centuries ago, noted how neighbors might agree to drain a meadow but how a thousand persons cannot agree since each will try to lay the whole burden on others. Magistrates are therefore needed who reflect the interests of "any considerable part of their subjects . . . thus bridges are built by the care of the government which tho' compos'd of men subject to all human infirmities, becomes, by one of the finest and most subtle inventions possible, a composition, which is, in some measure, exempted from all these infirmities" (Hume [1739] 1911, 539).

Adam Smith as well squarely recognized the need for state action in the provision of public goods. The prince, under the system of natural liberty, need no longer superintend the industry of private people, but he is still needed. That system leaves him with three duties, "duties of great importance indeed, but plain and intelligible to common understandings" (Smith [1776], 1937, 651). They include protection against invasion from abroad and a system of justice to protect against injustice and oppression from within. Third, there is the duty "of creating and maintaining certain public works and certain institutions, which it can never be for the interest of any individual, or small number of individuals, to erect and maintain; because the profit could never repay the expence to any individual or small number of individuals, though it may frequently do much more than repay it to a great society" (Smith [1776], 1937, 651). Externalities and the need to deal with them are recognized as part of the system of natural liberty. John Stuart Mill in turn pointed to important public services such as those of lighthouses that are to be performed by government, "yet there is no individual especially interested in performing them" (Mill [1848] 1985, 342). Public goods, as shown in these passages, had a firm place in the early stages of classical economics.

Two Models

The ground was prepared, but it took two centuries for Hume's "finest and most subtle invention" to be explored in rigorous form. Not much progress was made until the closing decades of the nineteenth century, when the advent of marginal utility analysis invited its application to public as well as private goods. Though differing in use (in my terms "rival" in the case of private and "nonrival" in the case of public goods), both should be provided so as to match the preferences of consumers with the cost of provision. The principle of equating marginal costs and benefits was to apply to both spheres, and the concept of public goods as meeting "state needs" was thereby set aside.

Starting from this common base, two lines of analysis developed. One strand, led by Wicksell (1896) focused on how such efficient provision could be arranged in practice. Given the free-rider problem and the resulting barrier to preference revelation, a political process of voting had to be substituted for bidding in the market. Thus public choice appeared as an inherent part of the fiscal process. The other strand, skeptical of the voting solution, postulated a referee to whom preferences are known and focused on the efficiency conditions to be met in dividing resource use between private and public goods (Samuelson 1954). By formulating the conditions for their efficient provision in analogy to but different from those for private goods, public goods assumed standing as members of the club and were given a legitimate place in the "hard-headed" world of Paretian economics. Both these models have been important to my view of public goods.

Essential though the efficiency model of public goods is as a theoretical construct, standing by itself it has little practical use. The omniscient referee does not exist and the problem of preference revelation must be addressed. The Wicksellian perspective is thus needed. A mechanism of mutual consent is required and takes the form of voting.

Since the terms at which public goods are available to any one individual depend on the contributions of others, this means that the expenditure and tax sides of the budget must be decided jointly. Wicksell thus proposed successive rounds of voting on program packages, combining specified expenditure and tax assignments. Since individuals must comply with the voting outcome, they have an incentive to make the best of the voting process. Following a voting rule of "proximate unanimity," a solution approximating benefit taxation is achieved. Individuals are left to contribute "tax prices," as Lindahl (1919) put it, in line with their marginal evaluation of the benefit. Taxation not only provides the government with the necessary means of finance but also serves as a mechanism to secure preference revelation.

Wicksell's model, to be sure, was overly optimistic. Transaction costs must be allowed for, as he himself noted though hoping that they would be minimized by advancing technology. Various forms of collusion, as Lindahl warned, may arise which interfere with efficient outcomes. Political as well as economic markets are imperfect. Alternative schemes such as point voting may yield superior results, and more complex approaches to preference revelation have emerged, whereby the expenditure choice is separated from its finance (e.g., Clarke 1977). Much remains to be done to improve budgetary procedures, but in the meantime the best available, if imperfect, forms must be used. Impossibility theorems notwithstanding, choice by voting, and with it a democratic process, is not a hopeless undertaking.

Mixed Goods

Both our models—Wicksell and Samuelson—address the central issue of what might be called "pure public goods," that is, goods whose benefits in consumption are nonrival and remain so whatever the number of beneficiaries may be. In that case, exclusion as a means of enforcing preference revelation and payment would be inefficient, even where feasible. Choice must be through a voting process. The situation differs for the case of "club goods," where exclusion can be applied and the common benefit falls as numbers rise (Buchanan 1965). Here exclusion becomes efficient, with marginal cost pricing offering a more marketlike mechanism of securing preference revelation. Nevertheless, a statelike role is still needed to organize and implement the club.

Another instance where a marketlike solution may apply arises in the case of externalities that involve small numbers. Where individual A generates externalities that impose costs on B, B may find it to his advantage to bribe A to cut back the damaging activity to an efficient level (Coase 1960). Or, in the case of external benefits, B may pay A to raise his activity accordingly. Thus external bads and goods may be privatized, and the "tragedy of the commons" is resolved without governmental intervention. That solution, however, is not feasible where larger numbers are involved so that individual members of the damaged or benefited groups will no longer find it advantageous to reveal their preferences in the bargaining process. The free-rider problem again raises its ugly head. Moreover, even where the damaged party can reach a bargain with the perpetrator, or the benefit-generating party can secure payment, there still remains the question of entitlement—that is, whether the perpetrator is entitled to pollute or whether the victim is entitled to be damage free. Government is again needed to set the entitlement rules. Allowance for mixed goods loosens the bounds between private and public provision, but the visible hand of government remains needed.

Public Goods and Communal Wants

The efficient provision of public goods in both our models rested on the premise of self-interested choice, with the difference between public and private goods arising from nonrival as against rival consumption. The tradition of German *Finanzwissenschaft* instead focused on differences in the underlying motivation by which goods are demanded (R. A. Musgrave 1997b). A distinction was drawn between self-interest-based choice in the one case and communal concern in the other. Thus individuals as members of the community may support (vote for) provision of certain goods—such as national monuments, the arts or education—as a matter of communal obligation, even though their personal preferences do not support them. At various times, I have tried to treat this motivation-based concept under the heading "merit goods" (R. A. Musgrave 1959, 1987b). Although I do not wish to assign merit goods thus defined a major role, I find it neither unrealistic nor shocking that communal concerns exist and that they might find such expression. At the same time, it should be noted that provision based on communal concern may involve private as well as public goods in the technical sense of rival versus nonrival consumption, so that the two perspectives should be kept distinct. Finally, the term "merit goods," as noted below, has also come to be used in a variety of other ways, for example, in the context of categorical equity and of nontradable goods.

V Equity and Distributive Justice in Fiscal Design

I now turn to my second key issue of fiscal design, that is, its concern with distribution. While some would prefer to exclude distribution since it falls outside the more manageable Paretian realm, this would leave the fiscal model in an incomplete state.

Efficiency and Justice: The Two Models Once More

From the Wicksellian perspective, the finance of public services may be approached via distributionally "neutral" benefit taxation, but for this outcome to be fair, it must be supplemented by securing a just state of distribution. For the resulting tax-expenditure arrangements to be just as well as efficient, as Wicksell noted, the underlying distribution of income must also have been just; to quote him, "*Gerechtigkeit der Besteuerung hat offenbar Gerechtigkeit der bestehenden Vermögens und Einkommensverteilung zur stillschweigenden Voraussetzung*" (Wicksell 1896, 143). Lindahl's contribution, entitled *Die Gerechtigkeit der Besteuerung* (Lindahl 1919), carries the same spirit. In order to close the model a tax-transfer budget has to be added to establish that just state of distribution; and, for this purpose, a social welfare function has to be defined. Arriving at that function involves issues that differ from those underlying efficiency in allocation as based on distributionally neutral benefit taxation. "Wicksellians" who feature the allocation part of his system while overlooking his premise of just distribution thus misinterpret his message. Wicksell, however, also counseled against interference with property rights and excessive pursuit of Wagner's redistributive use of taxation (Wagner 1893).

Distribution similarly enters when closing Samuelson's model. The referee first derives a utility frontier, showing Pareto-optimal combinations of mixes of public and private goods, together with distributions of private goods among consumers. As a second step, the optimal point on that frontier has to be chosen, and here a social welfare function is once more needed so as to determine what society views as a just state of distribution. Once more, the analytics of deriving that function differ from what is needed to derive the Pareto frontier.

Equitable Taxation

Contrary to the preceding models, traditional taxation theory—from Smith over Mill, Edgeworth, Pigou, and into modern optimal taxation—has viewed the issue of equity in the context of taxation only, independent of how the proceeds are to be used.

Focus, from Adam Smith on, has been on "ability to pay." As Smith put it, individuals should contribute "in proportion to their respective abilities; that is in proportion to the revenue which they respectively enjoy under the protection of the state" (Smith [1776], 1937, 777). He thus offered an intriguing formulation that may be read as combining benefit and ability considerations, but that linkage was soon dropped. From Mill on, justice in taxation came to be seen as justice in taking, to be arranged in line with ability-to-pay only. A just distribution of the burden was defined in terms of equality of sacrifice, and a triple distinction between equal absolute, proportional, and marginal sacrifice followed. While Sidgwick called for proportional sacrifice as the fair solution (Sidgwick 1874), Edgeworth and Pigou chose equal marginal sacrifice as the correct rule, a choice which, as Pigou put it (Pigou 1928, 43), was "given directly in intuition." With equal marginal equivalent to least total sacrifice, and least total sacrifice equivalent to maximum welfare, the paradigm was shifted from equity to efficiency, both joined in a single formulation. Based on the premise of comparable, equal, and declining marginal utility of income functions, the case was made for lopping off income from the top, a conclusion then to be qualified by allowance for what Pigou called the "announcement effects" of taxation, to be elaborated later as deadweight loss, and finally given a central position in the theory of optimal taxation.

Searching for the Social Welfare Function

Even after tax dollars and deadweight losses are counted, there remains the problem of how to value what is lost by particular people, a problem that must be met before optimal taxation becomes optimal. If, as now agreed, a Bergson-Samuelson social welfare function requires interpersonal and cardinal utility comparison, then an index for summing utilities is needed and the problem is how to derive it. With attempts to derive the function from normative axioms unsuccessful, attention turns to deriving it from a social contract. Self-interested individuals, still in the spirit of a Hobbesian bargain, are taken to agree on choosing the just state of distribution from behind a veil of ignorance, not knowing what their own position will be, and then render their choice on the basis of risk aversion (Buchanan and Tullock 1962). In a second, neo-utilitarian formulation, agreement to impartial choice is postulated as an ethical premise, but again followed by a risk aversion-based choice (Harsanyi 1953, 1955). Still another formulation also adopts acceptance of impartiality as an ethical premise but then replaces choice by risk aversion with a requirement that certain basic principles of justice be met, including equal liberty for all and maximin (Rawls 1972).

Among these various formulations of the veil model, I find the first unconvincing. Why should self-interested indi-

viduals, when knowing of their superiority, agree to an
impartial choice, even though still in a Hobbesian setting
they could secure a better bargain? Acceptance of an ethical
premise of impartiality, not to be derived from self-interest,
is thus needed to sustain the veil model. This is accepted in
the second formulation, but once the premise of equal worth
is given, it is not evident why this should have to be followed by self-interested choice based on risk aversion. Reasoning in terms of risk aversion, to be sure, is attractive to
the economist's penchant for maximization, but I question
its usefulness as a principle of justice. I thus find the third
formulation more congenial, although even here I wonder
why the construct of choice from behind the veil is needed,
once the premise of equal worth is already accepted.

I am also troubled by the veil construct if taken to mean
that decisions on distribution are to be made once and for
all in the original position or "constitutional" state. Distributional issues continue to arise over time and in new forms.
Moreover, observers such as myself who tend to be egalitarian should not rule out the norm of Lockean entitlement to
earnings (Locke [1690]; 1960; Nozick 1974) as an alternative
criterion that also deserves consideration. Most people, I
suggest, would wish to assign some weight to both norms.
In the end, the shape of the social welfare function as an
instrument of social policy remains to be determined
through the democratic process.

VI Macropolicy

It remains to note my third area of fiscal concern—that is,
the place of the budget in macroeconomics and policy. When
I came to Harvard as a graduate student, my interest in
public finance centered on the provision of public goods and
my dissertation was in that field. As I have noted at various

times, it was here that my acquaintance with the continental literature gave me some comparative advantage. At the same time, the Keynesian revolution, then in its most exuberant days, changed the image of the field, overwhelming these traditional matters with macro considerations. The very term "fiscal policy" came to mean the use of fiscal instruments as tools of macro policy.

In the nature of the Keynesian model as then understood, fiscal policy was *the* instrument by which to overcome unemployment and to emerge from the depression. It occupied this unique role because unemployment was seen to result from a deficiency of aggregate demand. That deficiency would not be overcome by automatic adjustments in the market. Wages were downward rigid and, even if falling, would be paralleled by falling prices without raising demand in real terms. Declining interest rates similarly met a floor and increased money supply would be absorbed by an infinitely elastic demand for liquidity. Increased government spending, deficit financed so as to avoid offsetting deflationary effects of tax increases, offered *the* only available means to generate demand and thereby restore full employment.

Public finances had to deal not only with selective market failure in the provision of public goods, but also with a more general macro failure in maintaining full employment. The ogre of excess saving was seen as a more or less lasting and recurring feature of the market system. All this was the theme and driving force of Alvin Hansen's fiscal policy seminar, the birthplace of the multiplier and accelerator principles, and discovery (as we then saw it in our youthful enthusiasm) of what public finance, if not economics, was really all about.

A good deal has happened since, with respect to both macrotheory and performance. The emergence of Hick's IS-LM model formulated the relationship among the basic

Keynesian functions in a more general and flexible fashion, so as to permit varying levels of employment and reopen effectiveness of monetary policy. Fiscal policy, was thereby deprived of its unique position. Combating inflation became a policy concern along with preventing unemployment, and the Phillips curve entered as a link between the IS-LM model and inflation. Moreover, a static concept of full employment equilibrium was replaced by an equilibrium path of income growth.

While encompassing these changes, the "neoclassical" model of the mid-1960s nevertheless retained the strategic Keynesian features of a demand-driven system that would not necessarily equilibrate at full employment. This view and its reflection in standard econometric models even now continues to dominate policy thinking, as evidenced by the pronouncements by institutions such as central banks, treasuries or the International Monetary Fund. Rational expectations or real cycle models, which would void the need for stabilization policy and neutralize its effectiveness, have been unconvincing. While the economic environment in which the expanded IS-LM model plays out has changed, its internal logic and the essential Keynesian variables still offer the preferred approach.

Granted fiscal policy will affect aggregate demand and thereby economic performance (be it employment or inflation), but the question remains what form it should take. As offered in Keynes's *General Theory*, it was assumed that expansionary policy meant increased expenditures, without considering the alternative of tax reduction. Thereby Keynesian policy became associated with increased budgets, an error later corrected by inclusion of tax reduction and built-in cyclical stabilization. Along with the choice of instruments by which to operate fiscal policy, the neoclassical model also offered a choice between monetary and fiscal action to affect aggregate demand, thereby linking control of aggregate demand to the composition of output between consumption and investment. That in turn placed the role of fiscal policy in the context of economic growth.

VII Conclusion

As these various dimensions of the fiscal system are combined, my primary concern has been with constructing a normative model of what a well-behaved public sector should look like. Along with this, I have been concerned with how such a model could be made to function, as a matter of empirical interest and because a balance of private and public concerns is needed to make society work. This necessity, as I see it, is not an unfortunate failure of creation. On the contrary, the existence of externalities and the need to confront issues of distribution enrich social life, the challenge of freedom and with it the human status of its members. The public sector as the instrument by which to address these concerns therefore constitutes a vital social capital, complementary and not rival, equal and not inferior to the market.

1.4   Discussion

Sinn: These have been two fascinating lectures and now we have some time for questions. Please feel free to ask whatever you think you would like to be answered.

Alan Williams, University of York, England: I wonder whether I could test both of our speakers by asking them whether there is some common philosophical position in which they could locate themselves but diverge somewhat within it. I would want to suggest, but it may be heresy to both of them, that deep down they are both rule utilitarians. That is to say, neither of them believes that by setting up some social welfare function alone, without any constraints, you can solve the problems that they are addressing. Nor do they believe in rules that have intrinsic merits irrespective of their outcomes. Therefore, I wonder whether it is a correct inference that they are, deep down, both rule utilitarians.

Musgrave: We both agree that for society to function there have to be rules, there has to be a legal order, there have to be strictures that relate to permissible behavior. But the function of rules, as I see it, is not only to restrain but also to enable. It is a matter of balance. The function of rules is to provide a framework that will restrain behavior harmful to the constructive interaction of individuals in society. But it is also the function of rules to enable, to bring such constructive interaction about. Therefore, I don't take the view that the function of rules is only to restrain; it is both to restrain and to enable. The problem is how to arrive at a proper balance between the two. At the same time, I am not a rule utilitarian. There are some basic ethical precepts that I would like to think western society accepts such as the *categorical imperative,* and the role of rules is to bring about their application. The rules serve outcomes. I thus like James Buchanan's new idea calling for rules that set up a domain of acceptable results. He thus allows for my view that rules have to be designed to bring about outcomes and that these outcomes are not arrived at from rules. There are underlying ethical precepts that should be agreed upon by society, not simply rules of procedure.

Buchanan: I want to go back rather than engage Richard Musgrave directly on the points he raised that no doubt will come up later on. Let me try to respond more directly to Alan Williams's question and query. I think the feature of both of our positions that is common, and I have underlined it in the lecture that Richard Musgrave gave earlier [is that] namely we are both basically contractarians. We are strictly within the contractarian part of political philosophy in the sense that we are really deriving everything from individuals as participants sharing in the collectivity. Where we differ, of course, is where we are within that tradition. We differ in that tradition in how we organize the sharing enterprise. More specifically to the question about rule utilitarianism versus act utilitarianism, I am certainly closer to rule utilitarianism than act utiliarianism, but I don't like to acknowledge that I am a utilitarian at all. But neither am I a complete deontologist either. It seems to me that Alan Hamlin wrote a very good dissertation with Alan Williams and Jack Wiseman and others, as I remember, in which he was looking critically at this whole question. He came out finally, if I understood it right, with the idea that, ultimately, even if we say we are interested only in structure and rules, they would have to be based on some predictions about patterns or consequences. So we can never get away from consequentialism in one sense. On the other hand, my own position is that I would rather hedge that just a bit; so I am both a consequentialist and a nonconsequentialist. I don't like to put labels on this. To get back to the discussion that we will be having here with Richard Musgrave, I think it does depend on the way we look at the potential and the dangers for shared enterprise. We put different weights on these two sides of the equation and we will be discussing that a good deal.

Frans van Winden, University of Amsterdam: We have had a very nice historical sketch of the development of public finance and public choice and, of course, we saw some philosophical roots uncovered. Now, we know that originally there was, one could argue, only one social science that gradually has been split up into different specializations, like economics, psychology, and sociology. I would like to ask our celebrated speakers about their opinion on this increasing specialization. The reason why I am asking this question is that I do not hear so much from them about the usefulness of insights that have been developed in psychology or sociology. There is more reference to philosophy. Are the other social sciences useful to our understanding of economic phenomena and, if so, what is the opinion of our speakers about the continuing specialization? Wouldn't it be useful to see to some kind of merger between these disciplines?

Musgrave: We probably agree that the various branches of social science have to interact, but they also develop methods and techniques that are suitable to their particular fields, but not to others. I am for interaction in that any particular problem involves many facets and requires different techniques but am bothered by the imperialism of economists, who use their tools on problems that are outside economics. I think, for instance, you find that in economics and law. There, economic tools are appropriate in some areas, such as torts, but not in others that involve concepts of justice and entitlements. Any particular problem, such as automobile accidents, may be viewed from the point of view of economics, of entitlement, of technology, and so forth, and they differ in each case. All these various dimensions should be considered, and they cannot be separated. But interaction should not take the form of applying techniques that belong to one area to others where they do not. Economics, of all the social sciences, is the only one that has a powerful mechanism of analysis, and so we can go and overwhelm the others that have no comparable engine of analysis. In that sense, I would question interaction.

Buchanan: I don't think the two of us differ a great deal on much of this. I have never personally been too concerned about this delineation of the specialties within the social sciences. I don't care whether I am acting as an economist or a political scientist or a sociologist, or what it might be if the problem seems interesting and it seems possible to say something about it. I have never paid much attention to disciplinary boundaries as a constraint on what might be worth researching, and I again mention the Max Weber point I made in my remarks. It seems to me that the differing approaches coming from different disciplines can, in fact, each contribute something. None of them are inclusively explanatory and I agree with what Richard Musgrave says in criticism of some of the modern economists who really try to argue that somehow economics gives you the total picture. You can say that the standard economic man assumptions give you a very important insight into a lot of behavior. But it is a big leap from that to say it gives you the only insight. I think that is something you have to be careful about. So I don't think there is a great deal of difference between us personally on that particular issue.

Sinn: We still have a whole week for discussions, and we should at some stage terminate. But there are still two questions. The first one is from John Komlos.

John Komlos, University of Munich: Mr. Musgrave spoke, of course, very eloquently of concepts such as justice and fairness, and I have a feeling that the two of us could agree on what we both consider just and fair in a particular situation. Unfortunately, I have not had the same kind of luck in convincing my son to think of fairness in the same way as I do in many different circumstances. So I was wondering if you would say a few words about what your conception of these two concepts is. How does one move toward a just society? Perhaps, if there is time, Mr. Buchanan could respond as well. Thank you.

Musgrave: I take it that your son as yet has not run away from home, so that he does not consider your sense of fairness so intolerable that he would not put up with it and vice versa. So it may not be as bad as all that. There are, of course, many different dimensions of fairness, and that which most enters into economics is the distribution of income and wealth. One of the fascinating developments in the United States, and I guess also elsewhere, is that there are now so many different dimensions in which these issues of fairness arise, such as in the treatment of race, of gender, of sexual preference, and so on, which all carry dimensions of what is right and what is fair, beyond matters of income distribution. Fairness is thus a very general problem. As for its economic dimension, my general sense largely agrees with Rawls in saying that inequality is fair only where it is to the benefit of everyone. But I also think that entitlement to earnings, the *Lockean* and Adam Smith tradition, has its merit. I would give it, say, one-quarter weight with three-quarters to the *Rawlsian* concept. Individuals in society have their own differing sense of fairness. It is therefore futile to say that there is one right definition that can claim absolute validity. But for society to function, it has to be sufficiently cohesive so that some degree of consensus can be reached. I don't mean this to call for defining fairness by majority vote, but for individuals to start out with equal inputs and equal voice into what is to be considered fair in society. If society has a commonly shared culture, it will reach some form of agreement.

Buchanan: Well, I won't comment on the larger set of issues here. There are a whole lot of issues which could be raised. We could spend a lot of time on it. I would just say this in relation to your comment about your son. I think we might learn a great deal from your son. Your question reminded me of some of the experimental work of early Piaget and other studies with children. Children do have a certain sense of fairness and as I remember Piaget's experiment, if you observe small children at play, they establish rules in which they do have these elementary notions of fairness, and we might learn a great deal from that. I think a lot of the problems arise when we push beyond those elementary notions of fairness that we can get from those perceptions on the part of children. There you get into genuine problems and then again it is pretty largely an empirical question as to what people do think of as fair. It is not us imposing our conceptions but what do people think of as fair. And there, you know, I am on board with the Rawlsian enterprise; at least he was aiming at the right way of trying to get at that question of how might people think of this rather than trying to impose and say this is what I think is fair or somebody else thinks is fair. The problem with the Rawlsian enterprise is, of course, that he should never have come out with a specific result. I mean, procedural justice as fairness in his original articles was right on target—that is, it is a process and you define justice by what comes out of the procedure. Rawls made a critical mistake by trying to come out and say this is what that procedure would generate. It won't necessarily generate the difference principle. The difference principle is perfectly legitimate as one possible outcome of a procedure, a fair procedure, but other things might have also come out and that is in part an empirical question as to what people do think of, in fact, as fair.

Sinn: The next question comes from Fritz Schneider, University of Linz. Maybe it could be short and the answers could also be short.

Fritz Schneider, University of Linz: It will be very short because my intended question has partly been answered. In the topic "The Nature of the Fiscal State: The Roots of My Thinking," you didn't deal very much with what you touched on now in the discussion: how you were influenced by empirical facts, especially by experimental economics. You could, for example, say that people do not engage in as much free riding as our theory would predict. They do not free ride in every case contrary to what theory would predict. Did this influence your work and does this kind of evidence from empirical economics influence it?

Buchanan: That's a very good set of questions. I think it is mysterious and I don't think we really know how accumulation of empirical findings or observations will in fact feed back to change our basic paradigms or our theories. I don't think we really know. It is mysterious. No doubt it happens. No doubt there is that feedback but I think in many cases people are very stubborn in giving up their theories in the face of empirical facts. Again, I would come back to what I said earlier, or related to what I said earlier, and take the free-rider problem. When you mention the experimental evidence, you are quite right: it suggests that people do not free ride as much as they would seem to if we plug in the hypothesis that people followed narrowly defined self-interest. But why would you really ever expect it to? It seems to me that the model in which people free ride is a model that gives us some insight into behavior. It does not, and no one should have ever claimed that it is a fully explanatory model. Now, in that sense, the empirical evidence really just tells you what the limits of the explanatory model are. It is more limited than might have been predicted but I think economists (and I think this is a real criticism of a lot of the empirical economists) implicitly plug in models for behavior that never should have been plugged in as being descriptively complete. They must do it in a certain sense in order to test these hypotheses that they try to test, but it pushes you way beyond the limits of the explanatory power of the underlying models.

Musgrave: Knowledge about how people behave under alternative circumstances is certainly a valuable input for designing rules. In order to establish a meaningful rule, one should know how people would behave if that rule did not exist. And to the extent that that can be established, or better explored through experimental economics, it is certainly a valuable input.

Sinn: Yes, thank you very much. I think this was a good start for today. It was not really a controversy because everyone explained his personal history. Tomorrow we will start with a real controversy, I promise you, and we will see how that will go.

Day 2 (24 March 1998)

2.1   Fiscal Tasks

Richard A. Musgrave

I Introduction

The basic functions of the fiscal state—the provision of public goods, concern with distributive justice and contribution to macropolicy—have been noted in my first lecture and their rationale need not be reconsidered here. Instead, I will focus on selected policy issues that have to be resolved. In the process, the three functions overlap but do not lose their underlying and distinct logic.

Problems worthy of consideration abound. Has public-sector growth reached too far and must it be retracted? Does the public sector strengthen or retard economic growth? Are public bureaus and their staffs productive? Should government be engaged in production? Why do public budgets offer private as well as public goods? How are pollution and other public bads to be controlled? How is poverty to be dealt with and how is social insurance to be adjusted to demographic change? What is good taxation and is there a need for drastic tax reform? Do budgets still matter as active tools of macropolicy? Brief comments on these issues will be offered, and many more could be added.

II Has the Public Sector Grown Too Large?

As one looks back at the course of the Western world during this century, public-sector growth has been one of its decisive features. The share of GNP flowing through public budgets in industrialized countries rose from about 10 percent at the beginning to an average level of 40 percent at its close, ranging from around 30 percent at the lower end of the scale (Japan, Australia, and the United States) to around 60 percent at the top (France, Denmark, and Sweden). With most of the expansion during the second half, various countries moved at different paces, but the trend held throughout the Western world.

Wagner's prediction of expenditure growth (Wagner 1893) was thus proven correct, even though half a century had to pass before it reached its full stride. That growth, as he argued, was not a random event, but a "law" traceable to three major factors; structural changes in the economy, democratization of society, and an increased concern for social justice. Rising interdependence among sectors of the economy, urbanization, and technological change would expand the need for public services. The decline of the self-sufficient agricultural household and of the family as a self-supporting unit would add thereto. In addition, Wagner expected the cultural and welfare concerns of society to broaden in the process of civilization, requiring increased attention to issues of distribution and Sozialpolitik.

There is thus an impressive array of "legitimate" factors to explain why the public sector should have grown. An alternative perspective views government as a self-aggrandizing Leviathan. Budget growth, or much of it, is seen in pathological terms, reflecting the fallacies of majority voting, the usurpation of power by self-serving politicians and bureaucrats, and fiscal illusion. I am skeptical of that model (R. A. Musgrave 1981a). Majority rule may cause the budget to be too small as well as too large, politicians may lead as well as abuse—fiscal illusion as well may work either way. Voters may think that they will receive benefits without cost, but they may also believe that taxes are paid in vain. Suffice it to say that while fiscal abuse may have been a factor, it surely has not been the major one.

With public-sector growth to be seen in its broad socio-economic and cultural context, it is difficult to assess the importance of particular forces. A brave attempt to measure the share of U.S. public-sector growth attributable to economic variables (income, population, structural change) accounted for less than half of the total (Borcherding 1977) but then erred in simply attributing the residual to distorting politics. Changes in the distribution of political power and institutions as well as changes in social attitudes are also legitimate factors that must be accounted for.

I do not wish to argue that public-sector expansion has been optimal and that policy determination has been without flaws. Of course it has not. But I do suggest that by and large expansion has been a necessary and constructive development. The growth of infrastructure such as highways, public education, and the rise of social insurance made essential contributions to economic growth and social well-being. A sound and strong public sector is needed along with the market to let society thrive. One cannot do without the other.

Public services, like private outputs, are not costless and both must be paid for. Taxes must be raised to provide the finance, and even though individual projects may seem worth their while, tax bills add up and deadweight losses rise well ahead of marginal rates of tax. The optimal size of the public sector with finance by lump-sum taxation would be one thing, but that with income or even value-added taxation is another. There is thus a limit to public-sector size in the context of a market system, but that limit is not rigid or easily established. Budget shares in GNP have varied widely across countries, reflecting different circumstances and social philosophies. Looking ahead, the goal should be to improve on performance rather than to cut back.

III Issues in the Provision of Public Goods

The most urgent problems now to be faced by Western budgets relate to transfers, but some issues pertaining to the provision of public goods will be noted first.

Consumption and Investment

The features that call for certain goods to be provided publicly, be it nonrival consumption or their nature as club goods, extends over both consumer and capital goods. The popular critique of government as "spender" or consumer, as against the private sector as saver and investor, is mistaken. The share of government expenditures on goods and services that flows into investment, especially if human investment in education and health is included, typically exceeds the investment share in private outlays. Moreover, the nature of certain public investments such as transportation, education, and scientific advance is especially strategic to economic growth.

It is important, therefore, that budgeting procedures distinguish between capital and current outlays. Whereas current outlays should be subject to the discipline of pay-as-you-go finance, economic logic—as I argued in my first publication (R. A. Musgrave 1939)—calls for the case of capital budgets to be loan financed, along with economic depreciation over the life of the asset. A balancing rule for the entire budget is bad economics.

Public Bureaus

Government cannot function in the abstract. Public bureaus and their staffs are needed to administer programs and assist in their design. The voting public, their representatives, and executives need expert advice on the costs and benefits involved.

For this purpose, a massive array of data has to be provided, furnished on a continuing basis and subjected to analysis. Cost-benefit analysis—one of the great contributions to constructive public-sector economics—provides a framework for program design. As elsewhere, the instrument is not perfect. Choice of the appropriate rate of discount is controversial and a direct measure of benefits is frequently unavailable. Analysis may have to be limited to compare the costs of alternative measures that yield equal results. Nevertheless, much is gained in the process. Engaged in these tasks, civil servants (in Weber's honorable sense of the term, as distinct from "bureaucrats" with its now derogatory connotation) perform an important function. It is in this context— the need for administration and policy guidance—that the state as bureau of public policy assumes an identity of its own similar in spirit to the mercantilist image of an efficiently conducted public household.

Public Production

As noted in my first paper, the task of the fiscal state is to arrange for the provision of certain goods and services that, because of their nature, cannot be provided by the market.

This requires public outlays and financing but establishes no presumption that the actual production should be carried out by government. Private companies can be hired to construct public roads. Private versus public provision, as I use the term, has nothing to do with private versus public production. The fiscal state is not a socialist order, a basic distinction that must not be confused.

Given a private enterprise economy, there is a presumption that production is handled best by private firms. But exceptions arise. Public production may become appropriate, where private production calls for close supervision, leaving the distinction between the two a matter of expediency. The pricing of natural monopolies, when operated privately, calls for public regulation, and establishments that generate dangerous externalities must be controlled. The nature of the required product, where publicly provided, may be difficult to specify when contracting with private producers. Farming out production is straightforward in the case of highways but can become highly complex in other instances, such as schools, prisons, or the courts. The quality of the product in itself may become a matter of public interest, an aspect of publicness not dealt with here but distinct from that of jointness in product use. Nevertheless, a presumption exists that the production of public goods should be contracted out, and that this could be done without restricting the scope of the fiscal state as here defined.

Public Provision of Private Goods

As we look at modern budgets, we find substantial inclusion of items that seem to be in the nature of private, rather than public, goods. Why should this be the case? Various explanations may be offered.

1. Certain goods, such as education or health facilities, provide personal benefits to the recipient, benefits that are rivals in consumption and not shared by others. In addition, they also generate externalities that the individual beneficiaries overlook. Supply forthcoming in response to private demand will be suboptimal, and a public supplement is in order. This may be provided by subsidizing private purchases or by public provision.

2. Provision in kind may be called for to meet essential needs of indigents or children, in settings where their guardians or parents cannot be relied upon to administer cash supports.

3. Provision in kind may be appropriate in the case of essential but scarce goods, or of goods highly inelastic in supply—for example, rationing of essential foods in wartime, allocation of scarce medicines to the most needy cases, or, in some urban settings, the provision of public housing.

4. These specific circumstances, however, are not the entire story. More generally, public provision of private goods may be taken to reflect a public attitude that views distributional justice in terms of categorical equity or "selective egalitarianism" (Tobin 1970). The availability of minimum levels is seen not in terms of income at large, but restricted to "essential" items of consumption. The social welfare function may thus take a paternalistic form, contrary to the standard utilitarian model of welfare maximization, calling for cash transfers and the use of proceeds in line with the recipient's own preferences.

5. A similar outcome may be arrived at in the context of Pareto-optimal redistribution, based on utility interdependence. The utility derived by donors may then depend on prescribed uses of the proceeds by the recipient.

The rationale for public provision of private goods may thus take a variety of forms. Beyond this, there is the further problem of effective implementation. In-kind provision of fungible items such as clothing or food can be readily diverted into other uses, while directed uses of low-cost housing or educational facilities can be assured more readily.

Public Bads

As we have become increasingly aware in recent years, government has to be concerned not only with securing public goods where market provision would be deficient but also with retarding public bads that are not accounted for by the market. Just as external benefits are overlooked, so are external costs. Taxation of pollutants offers an appropriate fiscal remedy and also generates the welcome byproduct of reducing the need for distorting taxation elsewhere.

Regulatory cutbacks in pollution-generating activity offer an alternative technique, and trading of limited pollution rights can contribute to their most efficient use. Translated to an international setting, less developed countries may accept higher levels of home pollution in exchange for goods that they value more highly, while developed countries may reduce their pollution at what they consider a worthwhile cost. Though efficient in economic terms, this leaves an element of unease, as a case can be made that the benefit of pure air be viewed in entitlement or categorical terms. Much also depends on how the distribution of pollution is determined.

IV Transfers

As previously discussed, the primary problem of modern budgets lies with transfer programs. Returning to the case of the United States, the expenditure to GNP ratio rose from

7 percent in 1902 to 25 percent in 1950 and 34 percent in 1995. Over the first half of the century, transfers contributed 22 percent of the rise in the ratio, while over the second they accounted for the entire growth, with the nontransfer ratio showing a decline. Since transfers leave the use of resources in private hands, this should please critics of government, who fear the potential waste of resources in public outlays. At the same time, the rise of transfers reflected an increased concern with issues of distribution and hence raised the weight of central budgets. The increase in transfers took various forms, including the two major contributing programs, poverty relief and social insurance, which will be briefly considered.

Relief of Poverty

Views on distributive justice differ and few would be willing to insist on full application of a maximin rule, but there is wide agreement that a safety net is called for and that some minimum should hold. The problem is how to provide it efficiently. The best solution is preventative: for example, education, a buoyant labor market, and adequate child care facilities. But direct support is needed as well. If meant to benefit low-income individuals in particular, welfare payments must decline as earnings rise and thus impose a significant marginal rate of tax on earnings. It is not surprising, therefore, when welfare recipients respond like millionaires and work less. An alternative approach would offer a universal demogrant financed by a flat-rate tax. The net effect would be a decreasing subsidy with rising earnings at the lower end, turning into a net tax higher up. Deterrent effects on work effort at the lower end might thereby be reduced, but at the cost of a high volume of fiscal churning. If the policy goal is to provide relief to the poor, why should the rich be permitted to share in the expenditure side of the program?

However formulated, relief of poverty must by its nature be a selective, not a general policy. To illustrate, let there be three people, L, M and H, earning $10, $50, and $100, respectively. Suppose further that the policy goal is to assure a minimum income of $15. Under a selective program, M and H will be taxed at 3.33 percent to raise the required revenue of $5 from a base of $150 with $5 then transferred to L. L gains $5, while M and H lose $1.67 and $3.33, respectively. Under a general program, all three receive the same grant and pay at the same rate of tax. In order to leave L with a net income of $15, a revenue of $18.46 is required. With a tax base of $160, this calls for a tax rate of 11.54 percent. L pays $1.15 and after receiving $6.15 is left with $15 as the program requires; M pays $5.77, receives $6.15, and is left with a net gain of $0.38; H pays $11.54 and after receiving $6.15 suffers a net loss of $5.38. A net benefit is extended to M who was not meant to be assisted, and a tax rate of 11.54 percent is needed rather than one of only 3.33 percent.

Used more recently, a vanishing wage subsidy given in the form of a tax credit for earned income has offered a novel solution, designed to dampen adverse effects on work effort but not applicable to non-earners. Further incentive problems arise where benefits are limited to single-headed families with children, issues that I expect will be discussed further in our final session.

Social Insurance

I now turn to social insurance, the second major transfer problem. As noted earlier, I hesitate to view distributive justice in terms of risk avoidance and insurance against uncertainty. Its basic problem arises even in the absence of uncertainty and has to be addressed first. Nevertheless, uncertainties also exist and call for the spreading of risks by insurance.

Old age insurance to meet uncertainty regarding length of life and the need to provide for retirement is the prime example. Prudent individuals will wish to insure and there are various reasons why public policy should be involved.

First, it is in the public interest that all individuals be required to insure. If left to their own volition, the reckless may abstain, leaving it to the prudent to bail them out later on. A minimum level of insurance, whether private or public, has to be made mandatory to protect against free riding. Second, society's view of distributive justice holds that protection against certain risks should be available on equal terms and adverse selection be avoided. Third, society, as a matter of categorical equity, may wish to subsidize the cost at which a basic level of insurance is available to low-income individuals. Finally, provision for old age insurance is a matter of public concern because it carries important implications for macropolicy.

To meet these concerns, there is a good case for a public system, so as to avoid the cumbersome regulations needed under a system of mandatory private insurance and to anchor social insurance as a shared concern. Some difficulties must, however, be resolved.

A public system of social insurance, in a setting of stable population, can be conducted on a pay-as-you-go basis and (disregarding its impact on the first generation), without raising problems of intergeneration equity. But with aging population, reserve accumulation is needed to avoid unfair burdening of the younger generation. This occurs automatically under a system of mandatory private insurance, where each beneficiary builds his or her own reserve. A public system, in turn calls for a pooled reserve, with insurance contribution and benefit claims set by statute. Long-term predictions of economic and demographic prospects are needed and when proven faulty require periodic revision. Due to a previously unexpected decline in population growth, social security systems in many countries are now confronted with deficits and a need for retroactive adjustments, changes that are difficult to make.[1]

Public insurance also poses the problem of how reserves are to be held. Under the public system, investment is typically in public debt, carrying lower yield but also involving less risk than does investment in private issues. Such prudence is appropriate for a system of social insurance, and a publicly guaranteed system of mandatory private accounts would also have to limit investment to less risky issues.

Critics of the public system, in turn, have questioned the practice of investing social security reserves in public debt. Since that debt must be serviced by the future generation, will this not void the very purpose of funding, which is to let each generation support its own retirement? This concern is valid if the funds made available by a surplus on social security accounts leads the government to raise current outlays or to reduce taxes. But the critique is not valid if the surplus funds are used to reduce the level of publicly held debt, thereby permitting increased private

---

1. An alternative approach, not dependent on economic and demographic forecasts might be found in a flexible pay-as-you-go system, setting average benefits not in absolute terms but equal to a fraction, say 40 percent, of average working income net of retirement contribution. Adjusting that fraction, say, every five years, to changing levels of income, the scheme then adapts automatically to changes in productivity and population growth (R. A. Musgrave, 1981b).

investment, or if the funds are used for public capital formation. In that case, the future generation will draw on a higher level of income and thus be able to service the debt and thereby contribute to the support of retirees without incurring a net burden.

Related and even more difficult problems arise under health insurance. What level of care should be viewed a basic entitlement in categorical terms, and in what form should health care be delivered? The aging of the population again raises costs as the need for care rises with age, while the advance of medical techniques further increases potential benefits and insurance costs. Setting the share of GNP that should go to health care will be among the most important fiscal issues to be resolved.

V Tax Reform

While new fiscal problems continue to emerge, tax reform retains a top ranking on the agenda. Though on the downside of the public budget good taxation, as I argued before, is a key test of democracy and a major piece of social capital. Taxation, as Justice Holmes put it, is the price paid for civilization. Having filled what must be thousands of pages on this topic over the years, I am aware that there are no ultimate solutions and that the prospects, at the end of the century, are not good. Nevertheless, the battle was worth fighting and continues to be so.

Changing Perspectives

The vision of good taxation, held by my generation of tax reformers, was that of a comprehensive, accretion-based and progressive personal income tax (Schanz 1896; Simons 1950).

The corporation tax would be integrated with taxation at the personal level. General consumption taxes (such as a retail sales or, later, value-added taxes) were held in low esteem, with property taxation accepted as an instrument of local finance. The rationale for that model is familiar and need not be repeated here. Income tax reform in this spirit, combining base-broadening with rate reduction, is still on the table. The U.S. reform of 1986 offered such a model and was followed by similar reforms, some successful and some not, in various European countries.

More recently, new plans calling for more drastic change have emerged. Despairing of the feasibility of reaching capital income at the personal level, the Nordic countries have forsaken the principle of global-based income taxation and have moved to a schedule-based treatment of capital income, to be reached via a tax at the company level. Dissatisfaction with the complications of income taxation has suggested even more drastic reform proposals. One widely discussed proposal in the United States, the so-called Flat Tax, would combine a 17 percent rate, cash-flow-type company tax (imposed on sales minus investment and purchases of inputs) with an equal-rate personal tax on wage income. The combined base would equal that of a consumption-type value-added tax, but taxation of the wage component at the personal level would permit a personal exemption. Looking at that base from the income sources side, expensing of investment exempts from tax the normal return to capital. Rents would remain in the base, but so would returns to risk and superior entrepreneurship, the item that matters most for growth. Another widely discussed plan (the so-called USA or "unlimited savings allowance" tax) would leave wage income in the cash-flow base of a 10 percent company tax but then add a progressive and personal expenditure tax.

Three questions arise: (1) Should income be replaced by consumption as base? (2) Should progressive bracket rates be dropped? (3) Should the principle of personal taxation be sacrificed to gains in simplicity?

Choice of Base

The traditional case for income as tax base, including all its sources and uses, rested on the merit of income as a fair measure of ability-to-pay. There should be no discrimination between sources such as wage and capital income, nor uses such as consumption or saving. The new view (actually dating back to John Stuart Mill) holds that the value of income is in consumption only and that taxation should be neutral in its impact on how consumption is timed. To avoid interference, the tax base as seen from the "sources side" should include wage income only and interest should be excluded. Or, when seen from the "uses side," the base should equal current consumption, leaving (under certain assumptions) the same present value tax in both cases.

The case seems plausible at first, but questions soon arise. Substitutability involves not only present and future consumption, but also leisure. Not all income is consumed and what is left (i.e., gifts and bequests) should be included in the donor's base. In addition, allowance should be made for the utility derived from holding wealth prior to its consumption. A supplementary tax on wealth would thus be called for. Given these concerns, I am not persuaded that consumption is clearly the better base, or that, viewed from the source's side, taxation should be limited to wage income only while excluding what traditionally has been referred to as "unearned" income.

Principles aside, it is correct, however, that the consumption or wage base can claim an advantage of simplicity in application. In particular, it bypasses the difficulties of measuring capital income, such as the treatment of depreciation. If set at a flat rate, it may be treated in in rem form, via a consumption-type value-added tax and without resort to personal taxation. This simplification is lost, however, if taxation is to be personal and at progressive rates, as under a Fisher- or Kaldor-type expenditure tax, as also proposed under the USA plan. The tax must then be personalized, as any one taxpayer's entire consumption has to be combined in a single base. To do so, consumption must be traced through financial accounts and measured as the residual of cash proceeds minus net repayment of debt and net investment. That procedure opens new difficulties, such as differentiating between consumption and investment outlays and dealing with financial transactions abroad. The simplification case for the consumption base is thus strong if linked to an impersonal and flat-rate tax, but much of that advantage is lost in a setting of personal and progressive taxation.

Tax Rates

Turning to the flat-rate issue, a distinction has to be drawn between applying a single rate to the entire base and applying it after allowing for a tax-free amount. In the former case, the effective rate (tax as percent of base before exemption) will be proportional, while in the latter it will rise from zero and approach the bracket rate. The flat-rate tax with an exemption is thus progressive in its effective rate. The exemption in effect forms a zero bracket. Up to well above the middle of the income scale, it is this zero-rate bracket that dominates. Replacement of the flat rate with additional bracket rates, therefore, matters mostly over the higher end of the income scale.

It does not follow, however, that the use of rising bracket rates at the upper end is of no significance to taxpayers further down. If revenue is to be held constant, replacing multiple bracket rates with a flat tax will sharply cut liabilities at the top, while raising them below, and especially over the middle range. I do not wish to follow that course, especially in a setting where, as has recently been the case in the United States, the distribution of wealth and earnings has become increasingly skewed. Rising bracket rates should thus be retained to adequately reach higher incomes. As the work on optimal income taxation has shown, the case for high marginal rates at the top is not as strong as proponents of progressive taxation earlier on believed, but the difference between, say, a top rate of 40 percent and the flat rate of, say, 20 percent is still substantial.

Personal Taxation

In all, the best course may thus be to stay with the income base and to simplify its application. With major loopholes closed, the tax for most taxpayers could then be collected largely at the source. However, refunds would have to be given for an exempt amount, thereby requiring the filing of returns, if in simplified form. The full-fledged income tax would continue to apply over the upper range. This would simplify matters for most taxpayers, but simplification is not the only concern. Visible taxation and personal participation in the taxation process is important as a matter of fiscal discipline and, recalling my Wicksellian links, is needed also to assure fiscal discipline and to offer guidance in the conduct of fiscal affairs. Tax equity also matters. Compliance with taxation, to be sure, should not be more burdensome than needed, but it is absurd to think that tax compliance in a complex world can be costless. In taxation, as in other contexts, we pay for what we get and good taxation is worth its price.

Global Setting

Before leaving these comments on tax reform, a warning needs to be added. Reform can no longer be viewed as a domestic issue only. Globalization of the economy has changed the terms on which tax policy has to operate as well as the goals that it pursues. Fiscal competition, for better or for worse, has become a major problem, a topic to which I will return in my final paper.

VI Macropolicy

It again remains to note the role of fiscal affairs in macropolicy, the remaining major issue. Primary responsibility for macropolicy in my early years was assigned to fiscal policy. Monetary policy was considered ineffective. Changing conditions and theoretical insights have now moved monetary policy to the fore. Nevertheless, the macro aspects of fiscal policy still matter.

Macro Use of Fiscal Instruments

Budgetary shifts to deficit or surplus finance still affect aggregate demand, output, employment and inflation. The I.M.F. and U.S. authorities, notwithstanding their usual counsel for tight budgets, only recently demanded that Japan loosen its fiscal stance to reduce its trade surplus. Expectations do, of course, enter and indeed played a key role in the I and L functions of the Keynesian model; but the presumption that expansionary or restrictive effects of budget policy are washed out by anticipated effects on the future level of taxation is implausible. Consumers are not Ricardian scholars; and anticipation of policy effects, where it occurs, disturbs monetary as well as fiscal policy outcomes. The neoclassical model, on the contrary, still has much to be said for it. Such is the case even in a buoyant setting, and situations may again arise where adjusting interest rates will not be the all-powerful instrument of stabilization policy. Fiscal measures may again be called upon to play a more active role. This does not mean that the principle of balance in the current budget as a safeguard of fiscal discipline should be abandoned. Rather, it calls for rewriting the balancing rule in terms of baseline balance, leaving a degree of flexibility to meet changes in economic conditions as they occur. A rigid requirement of continuing balance, or even a firm 3 percent rule, is poor economics.

Interrelationships

While the macro role of fiscal policy continues to be of major importance, it must not be considered the only concern. Considerations of "functional finance" must also be reconciled with the more traditional aspects of public finance bearing on the efficient provision of public services and the efficiency/equity quality of tax policy. Expansionary measures may be undertaken either by way of raising expenditures or by reducing taxes, and different tax designs carry implications for both resulting changes in consumption and investment outlays as well as for the distribution of the tax burden, and with it for tax equity. It is appropriate for me to stress these interrelationships since my model of the fiscal system—including its allocation, distribution, and stabilization branches—requires such a comprehensive view of what in the end constitutes good management of the public sector.

VII Conclusion

My purpose in offering these brief comments on a variety of policy issues was to show how and why the contribution of the fiscal system is needed as a complement to the market and an equitable society. Emphasis accordingly was on what is needed and what can be done to meet these goals. Defining the good fiscal system, as I have felt over the years, should be our primary task, not because there are no policy failures but because first things come first. If we do not know how to do it right, how do we know what failures to correct? Nor is the task beyond the reach of a democratic society. I do not join Hume's proposition that in viewing government "everyone ought to be considered a knave" (as quoted in Brennan and Buchanan 1980, 34). I would rather draw on people's capacity to serve as responsible members of the community, so that government may do its important tasks and do them well.

2.2   Response

James M. Buchanan

Essentially there are two parts to Richard Musgrave's lecture this morning. The first part deals with the spending side, or the role of government, and the second with taxation, so let me separate these. In one sense, I think Richard Musgrave is to be commended and congratulated because it took a lot of courage, I think (and he deserves credit for this), for someone to get up and defend the status quo. That is essentially what he did in the first part of the lecture in terms of the growth of the public sector, defending the size of the public sector as it is now—especially as it has grown in the last half century.

There is a critical question about optimal size of the public sector. However, let me be clear; I am not willing to impose my own preferences here on that question. Whether or not citizens as individuals want to spend their resources collectively through joint action, or whether they want to spend them privately, is for people to decide themselves. I have never ever been, as I noted yesterday, an anarcho-capitalist who says the state should do nothing. I have never denied an efficiency-enhancing role for the collective agency, the state. Clearly the legal framework must be provided, to provide protection for property and contract, and that can

only be provided through a collective agency. I also think
that there needs to be some predictability provided in the
value of money and also some enforcement of a competitive
market. There is no quarrel between us on that point at all.
The dispute arises, I think, when we move beyond what I
call the realm or boundaries of the protective state into what
we might call the productive or transfer welfare state. As for
public goods, genuine public goods in the technological
nonrivalry sense, I think Musgrave acknowledges that relatively few of those exist. I have seen various estimates for
various countries, Scandinavia, Britain, and also the United
States, that suggest that if you stuck with public goods, even
in the broad definition of genuine public goods in the technological sense, you might justify a 10–12 percent share of
GDP being devoted to financing those goods. The problem
arises when you move beyond that to the collective provision of partitionable goods or private goods in the technological sense. I quite frankly have never understood, and I
have known Musgrave's work for more than four decades,
his notion of merit goods. I think you can make an argument
for having collective agencies subsidize particular types of
consumption from a paternalistic perspective. All of us in
one sense of the word sometimes like to think of ourselves
as paternalistic. I have never understood how that is fundamentally derived from a contractual basis. (My professor,
Frank Knight, whom I referred to yesterday, used to say that
he could never distinguish between opponents of the market
systems; some opponents objected to the market because the
market worked, and the other opponents objected because
the market failed.) You can take a market failure approach
and derive a logic for correction through political action. But
a lot of the opposition to markets comes about because
people don't like what people prefer. They don't like peo-

ple's tastes and, therefore, they want to impose a better standard. And, in a sense, there is an argument here but you have to shift into another model.

As to the distributional aspects, I think that is the hardest of all the problems. I agree fundamentally with some criticism that Musgrave has made in earlier works, and I agree with him that the problem here is the primary distribution problem. I think the so-called Pareto-optimal redistribution stuff is pretty much peripheral to the fundamental argument, which is how far you want fiscal redistribution to proceed. I don't buy at all into Nozick-type entitlement claims. Richard Musgrave and I share the same position on that. But I think you do have to make some distinctions here. You have to make a distinction between what type of distribution you would like to see or what type of distribution would be broadly acceptable, and how much *redistribution* you want. Those are two quite separate questions, and I think fiscal economists and others get them mixed up. Where you have to have politicized redistribution is quite a different thing from saying what would be an ideal distribution. My concern, of course, has always been, once you allow politics to get into the distributional element that you can't necessarily get what you might think would be desirable. You might even move in the wrong direction rather than the right direction toward a distributive norm, whatever than norm might be that you set up. I think Rawls was at least trying to get at some of those basic fundamental questions about deriving what would be the proper distributive norm. As I said yesterday, he might not have been successful, and I think he was being far too specific, but at least he was trying to get at some of the fundamental problems. And I do think if you throw transfers or redistributions openly into the political arena, you are almost going to guarantee class conflict or the churning state, and you are not necessarily going to get the distribution going from the rich to the poor or whatever you might like. I do think that somehow or another there is a legitimacy for some action by collective agency to maintain fairness in the game. But what does fairness in the game mean? I have always concentrated on equality of opportunity, and I have always thought that educational spending ought to be brought under that rubric rather than under any public goods rubric. It seems to me that that is a clear aspect of the equality of opportunity notion and I have always been in favor of fairly severe taxation of inheritance for that same reason, recognizing all the problems. But that is a fuzzy area. I don't think we have definite answers in the field of distribution.

Now let me get to the tax side. I am going to put off until tomorrow the discussion about the flat tax. Let me say only this: I have changed my views in the last decade. When I wrote *The Power to Tax* (Brennan and Buchanan 1980), as Richard Musgrave said, we came out in favor of a progressive tax from a constitutional perspective, and I was at that time very much opposed to the flat tax. I have come around to support the flat tax for different reasons, but I will leave that aside because I do talk about that in my lecture tomorrow. Let me talk about the recent events in tax history here, related to some of the things that Richard Musgrave said. The 1986 tax reform act in the United States was an act that was rather interesting in its origin. Nobody expected it to come out of a democratic process and it was a tax reform act that, rather surprisingly, was viewed as a major step in the right direction, in the proper direction, a desirable direction, by almost everybody in the tax business, whether you come at it from the far right, the middle right, the center, the mild left, or the far left. All across the spectrum, everybody thought that this was a great piece of legislation because it essentially closed up a number of loopholes. It lowered the rates, widened the base, and did exactly what Richard Musgrave and Joseph Pechman and others had been preaching for years. It swept in very quickly and it was a very good reform—it lowered the rates, basically to a two-bracket structure and really did widen the base considerably.

The editor of the *Journal of Economic Perspectives*, Joseph Stiglitz, asked me to write a piece assessing the 1986 act from a public-choice perspective. I wrote an article that was published in 1987 in the *Journal of Economic Perspectives* (Buchanan 1987). I am very glad I am on record with that piece because all of my predictions turned out to be precisely on target. Because I predicted from a public-choice perspective that Congress had exhausted the rents that it could get from selling loopholes. Therefore if it could sweep them all clear and cut the rates, it would then have the chance to raise more revenue by immediately starting raising rates again with a wider base, which is what Congress did. Second and more important, once Congress had wiped out all those rents, it could then start reselling the rents. And of course that is exactly what happened. The act was hardly cool off the presses when Congress started putting in new loopholes, new changes. It did that in the 1990 schemes, and it did that again in the 1992 schemes, and, of course, Clinton is doing that with abandon now. When they talk about targeted taxes and targeted programs, which is nothing more than selling loopholes for these rents. I am unhappy, as Richard Musgrave surely is, with what has happened since the 1986 act, but that is predictable, necessarily predictable, given the way we make tax policy. And I think if you come at this from a public-choice constitutionalist perspective, you do in fact get a totally different view on the whole fiscal state or fiscal structure.

Relating to *The Power to Tax*, let me just say one thing, and perhaps I will get into some of this tomorrow. We realized that Richard Musgrave and others were upset with that book, and, as I said, we wrote another book to respond to them, because we didn't think they had really understood our purpose. In a more general sense—and some of you may share Richard Musgrave's position on this—I think there is a fundamental difference between American and European attitudes, not necessarily only on taxation, but on what I would call an attitude toward constitutional structure. Europeans (and recognizing that Richard Musgrave comes out of a European tradition), I think, have a difficult time in comparison with Americans in understanding what we mean when we talk about constitutionalism. We naturally think, and I think this applies not only to the academic world but also to the world of the ordinary public out there, that Americans have a sense that constitutions are needed to constrain politicians. You don't really have that tradition, and in a sense that is the fundamental break between Richard Musgrave's position and mine. He trusts politicians; we distrust politicians. That is a natural, inherent part of our thinking. We don't get away from that. We can never get away from that. And if you find somebody who takes the other view, you almost say, well, somehow or other, he is European in his thinking.

I will end with a story. Sometime after *The Power to Tax* was published, and it illustrates this point I am making here, Richard Musgrave and I were at a conference somewhere, and I raised this question: Don't you feel that under certain circumstances, you would want to constrain the government? And I said, for example, suppose you had a tiger, a pet tiger. Wouldn't you want to have a muzzle on that pet tiger in case that he might bite somebody? So you put him on a muzzle. And Richard Musgrave said, oh I wouldn't want to do that because I might want the tiger to eat the grass.

2.3 Discussion

Sinn: So, is there more about tigers? Peter Bernholz, can you go to the microphone please?

Peter Bernholz, University of Basel: James Buchanan, first of all, I would reject your generalization about Europeans. I personally feel that I am very suspicious of the government and still I am a European, and I even think that it was a European who started the whole business of restricting the government. Second, the law should not be called Wagner's law because I found out by chance that Umpfenbach had suggested it before, so it should be called Umpfenbach's law. But that is only for the public-finance people. Now, turning to taxes, and the same is also true for expenditures, I think we have heard too much about what they *should* look like. From a public-choice perspective, I would prefer to ask what they do look like.

Now we start from the premise of rational politicians. What should politicians do if they want to hide the burden from the uninformed voters? They would, of course, try to minimize the voters' information. How can you do that? You introduce very many taxes so that nobody knows what the taxes are and then you introduce, for instance, deduction at the source for wage income so that people don't perceive that. In Switzerland, for instance, we don't have that system. We have no deduction of wage earnings at the base, so people resist tax increases far more because they are better informed. Thus, you might ask yourselves, what are the present-day tax rates for the different taxes? Do you know them? We don't know them usually even as economists, which goes to illustrate this point.

I would suggest that something similar is done on the expenditure side. It would be nice if all the transfers went to the needy, but I see that DM 100,000 are spent per year per worker on subsidies in the coal industry. In addition, we have all the subsidies in agriculture. The United States also had them. What do these subsidies have to do with redistribution toward the poor and needy? Nothing at all. So from a public choice perspective, you would first have to look at what the driving forces for this development are, and I think that some of James Buchanan's remarks are pointing in that direction. If we want then to design some optimal taxing and expenditure system, we should keep that in mind. I leave open whether it is to be more or less redistributive. Everybody has to make his own decision here. Nevertheless, in designing the tax, we have to take into account these tendencies of the government.

Alan Williams, University of York: I have three points I want to make. First of all, I was a little surprised that in your comments, Richard Musgrave, you didn't mention anything about Baumol's hypothesis relating to the relative growth of the public sector. He observes that there are sectors where there is great technological advance and other sectors whose activities have little scope for technological advance, and he believes that the latter gravitate into the public sector. And that would require more resources to be drawn into the less technologically advancing sector, even to maintain the same proportion of output. Now the trouble with the public sector is that we do not have good measures of its output, and we tend to assume that resources going in represent the value coming out (if we are optimistic), or (if we are pessimistic) a drain down which resources go to be lost forever. I think that, without independent measures of the output of the public sector, it is very difficult to answer the questions about what is the optimal balance between the public and the private sector. I think technically we are not up to making those judgments from within what we know in economics. Second point: I want to address the issue that James Buchanan rightly works on, which is why should we be in the game of collectively second guessing what will improve our lot as individuals, when maybe as individuals we could do it for ourselves? I mean, from a social perspective, why do we wish to constrain ourselves? I think the reason for that is that in the market, or in the individual day-to-day behavior, we tend to adopt rather short time horizons over our behavior, and yet we know that in many respects we ought to be taking a longer-term view of our own welfare. When you are very poor, you have to take a very short time horizon. It is the only way of surviving. As you get richer, you can take a longer time horizon. You can think more about the future, about education, for instance. Think about young people's behavior with respect to smoking. They don't expect the damage to hit them for some time, so they don't even think about it. When it begins to hit them, it is too late to think about it. Now it seems to me therefore that one could also see this issue not in a *cross-sectional* way, which is the way it is often looked at, of simultaneously having groups of people who are doing better and worse, but *intertemporally*—that what we are doing is redistributing results for ourselves between our short-term present and our long-term future. I think a lot of the material about public provision of pensions and health care has to do with that, and also education, because although there are many children who really enjoy being in school, I hated it, so a paternalistic parental element enters into it. My third point is about morality. There was a very interesting example of the impact of morality upon taxes in my university recently. The university finance officer came up with a very clever scheme whereby the university would pay less taxes and we would get more money if we adopted a device that was perfectly legal, and perfectly open, and had been agreed with the Inland Revenue. It was put to the vote as to whether we would accept this tax dodging device. The university staff voted 2 to 1 against accepting it, on the grounds that it was against the spirit of taxation and was antisocial behavior.

Ewald Nowotny, Vienna University of Economics: Perhaps in all fairness I should add I am also a member of the Austrian parliament. What I should like to invite are some comments on the connections between the size of the public sector and employment developments because this is a problem that is of great relevance especially for European countries now. If we compare the United States and European countries, the service sector in the United States, the people employed in services, is much higher compared to say Germany or Austria. A large part of this can be explained by activities that in the United States are privately done but in Europe are provided by the public sector: education, the health services, prisons, and so on. What we have now is the problem that in Europe we have the feeling we do not want to provide these services in private ways because it would have negative distributional effects. So we want to keep them in the government. On the other hand, the government has financing barriers, so we cannot finance any increase of these services. So what we have is a kind of institutional trap where, on the one hand, we cannot exploit the employment chances due to financial barriers and, on the other hand, we do not want to privatize. My question now is, what would your feeling be about getting out of this trap: Could we try to weaken this financing barrier—for instance, would some kind of earmarked taxes or some kind of fees for financing specific service activities of the public sector be what you have in mind? Or would you think that one has to accept that you cannot pursue distributive aims by means of public service provision of services, so that you would have to rely on direct money transfers with all the problems of income-related transfers. The possible connection between the financing barrier, employment, and the service aspects of the public sector is something I would like to hear more about.

Sinn: It would be useful in order to get more coherence into the discussion if Richard Musgrave answers this question right now.

Musgrave: All right. We shall talk more about taxes later on. Going back to the matter of merit goods, I know that they are a controversial concept, and I have also changed my view of them over time. I like to think of them in relation to the individual's place in society, not as an isolated person but as a member of his community. As such, he might support certain public services because they are seen as part of the community's cultural heritage, rather than in response to his private taste. Support of merit goods thus involves a form of social interaction that is not purely individualistic. I am well aware that once you get out of the safe haven of purely individualistic concerns, there are all sorts of dangers, but, as I said yesterday, I don't think that you can reject the concept of community values on those grounds.

Sinn: Thank you. Since you picked the merit argument, let me just personally add one thing here. If there are children, I think there is a merit good problem, right? You have to have a paternalistic approach toward these children. The question then arises: Should the parents themselves exclusively decide what resources should be given to the children, or should society have some say with regard to children? If you think that society also has some responsibility then you end up with merit goods arguments of the Musgrave type. But this is the only legitimate argument in favor of merit goods that I could imagine, and so far I have a lot of sympathy for what James Buchanan said.

Now we have more remarks. Please.

Hartmut Fest, Ministry of Economics: I am heading a task force on structural aspects of globalization. It has not been mentioned that one of the currently important contributory factors toward the growth of the transfer system could be globalization. I draw your attention to the work published last year by Dani Rodrik of Harvard. He has run regressions with several measures of openness of an economy as an exogenous variable and has found that there is a strong correlation between the size of the transfer system and openness in a number of countries. For certain subperiods and countries where the growth of openness has been very pronounced in the sixties, seventies, eighties—namely Austria, Netherlands, and Belgium—he suggests that governments reacted in a rational way to the pressures of an opening economy. They bought off interest groups that were mostly affected—that is, low skilled workers, coalitions attached to a sectoral interest; and so on. To be more exact, openness was not measured by export-import shares but by a measure of the volatility of terms of trade. After external shocks, one could easily observe this relationship. Isn't it a little bit ironic that German politicians point to Holland and the Dutch system as a shining example of how to solve the social problems associated with globalization? Now, if that is to be the model for Germany, we would have to anticipate further growth in the transfer system, exactly as Professor Musgrave has probably noted for the past. Would the two gentlemen please comment on this kind of work? When I mentioned Rodrik's work to Paul Krugman in the December session at the CES, he cut me short and said Rodrik doesn't understand the implications of what he was doing, and implied that most of the readers, including myself, didn't grasp it either. But I think for small countries, there may be a conclusive case that some governments reacted in such a way.

Sinn: We will come back to that on Thursday when we talk about fiscal competition. That is the right place for it.

Christoph Engel, Max-Planck-Group, Bonn: I, being a lawyer by training, could hardly contradict in principle your idea of categorical equity and, just to give you one example, if we are against human organs being traded on an open market, categorical equity must be the reason we give for that. Nonetheless, I have a few concerns with the idea of categorical equity and I would like to ask you how you feel about it. My first problem is, what are the categories for singling out items that should for philosophical reasons not be traded on markets? Let me give you a concrete example in this country. We are strongly opposed to trade in waste. My concern is that this might be hidden protectionism because in preventing waste from being disposed elsewhere, we are protecting our high disposal standards and thereby our waste enterprises. I think this is not an unusual example. Categorical equity is very easily misused as a disguise for rent seeking, and I would very much look for categories preventing people from just doing that. And a last point, am

I correct in thinking that your overall scientific system might be based on the idea of categorical equity—that this is in a way the cornerstone of your scientific thinking and not textbook economics?

Sinn: I think that this is a very important point and I would wish to ask if anyone else has something on this issue—categorical equity. If not, Richard Musgrave should briefly answer and maybe James Buchanan could add a few words.

Musgrave: It should not be too difficult to explain what categorical equity means. In its legislative form, a decision is made to give budgetary support to the availability of certain low-income services, such as low-cost housing or medical services. [*Voice from the audience:* Mining industry.] No, no. Making such grants should reflect the voter's view of equity that such services should be available to low-income households. If you begin with the proposition that equity in distribution is a social concern, there is the further question of whether this should relate to the distribution of income and the availability of goods at large, or only to items that society views as essential. While that may be viewed as interfering with consumer choice, society may wish to supplement measures directed at a fair distribution of income by further measures relating to particular areas of availability. The latter may permit limited use of the former and also serve to address special contingencies. Moreover, allowing for utility interdependence, the satisfaction derived by donors may well depend on how the transfer is used by donees.

Sinn: Thank you. I think categorical equity is something that obviously exists in the heads of the people, right? The general attitude is that everyone should have enough to eat, everyone should have a house to live in, and so on, but you don't want everyone to be able to go to Tenerife for a splendid holiday. People think like that. Whether it is a legitimate philosophical category that we should take for granted is a completely different question, and I would like to hear James Buchanan on this question.

Buchanan: I think the fundamental problem here, and I think Richard Musgrave was getting at it in the very last part of his comment, is the mixture of the normative with the positive. It gets us all very confused in a certain sense. And I think using the term *categorical equity* is not a good term here at all. It seems to me much better, rather than blanket this into some general normative concept, to look at it strictly from a positive point of view. This is getting at what you just said. Looking at it strictly from a positive point of view, people are willing to support other people in a redistributive sense if it is directed redistribution. The externalities, if you want to put it that way, the negative externalities exerted by people living in shacks that you see as you drive down the road will make you in fact support housing for those people whereas you would not support direct income transfers. So, in a positive sense, you can make an explanatory model that will give you some feel for why you observe: a good part of redistributive spending going in the form of these directed programs as opposed to trying to justify this through a grand categorical equity notion. I think it is much better to proceed in a more positive way and see how can you have an explanation for that which you observe.

Sinn: This issue, someone else? Directly related. OK.

Bernholz: My colleague, René Frey in Basel, some twenty years ago had empirical research done on the Basel theater. He found out among others that at that time, each ticket was subsidized by I think 75 or 78 francs and he also asked people about it. Now if you look at subsidies to theaters, you mentioned the opera before, shouldn't people be able to show their preferences? At the time, I told my colleague René Frey you should have asked the people attending the theater: Would you have gone to the theater if you would have been paid out these 75 francs otherwise? What would you say to this argument? Should we force them to go there with the subsidies despite that?

Sinn: I believe that this is an unfair comparison because no one has that in his mind when he talks about categorical equity. It is exactly the kind of category that Richard Musgrave does not mean. He means, of course, the basic needs that should be satisfied for everyone, not the opera visit. [*Voice in audience:* We went to the opera yesterday.] Yes, we were there yesterday. I hope you liked our subsidies. If there is nothing more on this I have two further people who would like to say something. The first is Gerold Krause-Junk.

Gerold Krause-Junk, University of Hamburg: I think both of our speakers agreed that the '86 tax reform was a great one in the sense of broadening the tax base and many countries over the world have tried to follow, including Germany this year unsuccessfully. James Buchanan says that after only a few years all the loopholes are creeping in again and that he predicted that. Assuming that we could predict the same thing now if we tried to do this in Germany, what kind of advice would you both give us? The first advice I could think of was to leave things be as they are, because although you could close all the loopholes, after some years, big surprise, all these loopholes are there again. The second advice you could give, or that I could think of, is do it once and for all and then change the constitution and say that income tax is no longer a policy matter. But what would be the consequences? Politicians then would need other subsidies or would use other instruments as we have heard, or other direct controls, and I wonder whether really all these other instruments are so much better that we should change the constitution and take income tax completely out of actual policy. So what would be your fair advice in a situation like this? Personally, I must say that I have the feeling this is a dynamic process, so to say. After a couple of years, let us say every twenty years, you have to sweep the carpet clean and then let the politicians try to implement their own ideas. Each generation has the right to have its own ideas about good policy; they can use the clean carpet and as long as we know that after a certain time we will clean it again, then everything is OK. This is a very pragmatic view, of course. I wonder what you have to say about this.

Sinn: Is there someone else on this issue—tax cut cum base broadening? There is one remark I would like to make. If you compare the 1981 and 1986 tax reforms, and this is for James Buchanan, you see exactly the opposite mechanism. The 1981 reform reduced the tax base by introducing the Accelerated Cost Recovery System. Later when firms had exhausted their depreciation possibilities, they went to congress to reduce the tax rates, and they did not mind broadening the base again. So it goes around all the time, right? It is a full circle. This is in line with what Gerold Krause-Junk said.

Musgrave: I would add to what James Buchanan said. The '86 base reform was followed by an increase in rates but that in turn was followed by further measures to weaken the base. Had the base not been improved in '86, what happened in '97 would have moved it back to its '81 position. Objecting to improvements because they may be wiped out later seems too pessimistic a point of view.

Sinn: Thank you, any further comments?

Frans van Winden, CREED, Amsterdam: I would like to comment on what seems to be a common understanding of James Buchanan and Richard Musgrave. I refer to the view, shared by many others, that real public goods should be provided by the government. The comment I would like to make is that one should be careful here in light of recent theoretical and empirical research. We know, for instance, from the work by Elinor Ostrom and others, that in the past people have taken care of common pool resource problems in many ways. We also know from our own experience that people do care, to some extent at least, about the environment in their own communities, or about crime and justice. Recent research on social capital shows that functional interaction, which typically happens in the context of the voluntary provision of public goods, can create social ties (utility interdependencies) and thereby social capital, with very important spillover effects. If people are in need, for instance, then they can rely on this social capital for help. This has important consequences for government policy. For example, if the government steps in by putting more policemen in the streets to take care of crime, then this may crowd out not only the private activities of individuals but also the social ties that have been built up, which can be very costly. Of course, I do not want to say that governments should not take care of public goods. But I think we should be more careful because of these social mechanisms.

Sinn: Is there anything on the crowding-out issue? I think this should be the last issue we discuss. There is, of course, the literature about the private provision of public goods, and this can show some crowding-out effects, but at what level? You have to see that the private provision of public goods leads to the provision that one individual would find optimal. In a large economy, this is close to nothing. We have just had a habilitation thesis on that issue here by Kai Konrad, which I advise you to read. We are talking about a level of provision of public goods that is definitely much less than the socially efficient level, and at that level there may be some crowding out effects. On that issue? I think we should give our speakers the opportunity to say a final word.

Musgrave: If people had a perfect mutual concern for each other, we would be in paradise and need no rules. And certainly it would be nicer to be in paradise where no rules are needed than to be in the real world where they are. Where public provision of public goods does, in fact, drive out what would be their private provision, nothing would be gained, but I don't really see much evidence of that. Public provision is more likely to be driven out by private resistance, such as tax evasion.

Sinn: I think the time has elapsed. Thank you all very much and, in particular, the speakers. This was a great day. We had a lot of good points and insights. I am looking forward to a continuation of our discussions tomorrow.

Day 3 (25 March 1998)

3.1 Constraints on Political Action

James M. Buchanan

I Introduction

The lectures and discussions in the first two sessions of this seminar indicate that Professor Musgrave and I approach the same subject matter, summarized as "the public economy" with substantially different visions or perspectives. As I discussed at the beginning of my introductory lecture in the first session, some of our differences can be traced to the separate windows through which we observe, interpret, and evaluate political reality, both as actualized and practicable potentiality. But we should be able to go beyond the straightforward statement of our differences here; we should be able to identify just where and how the differences may affect our ultimate judgments on organizational alternatives and particularly on proposed reform initiatives.

In his lecture in session 2, Musgrave presented his normative vision of the political or public economy, a vision that incorporates a positive analysis of just how such an economy works, again both as observed and imagined. My comments have already suggested that the collectivized or politicized sector of the inclusive economy in Musgrave's idealization (1) may not work as well as he has envisaged, and (2) even if problems of efficacy do not arise, the collective range of action in that idealization would, for me, remain too intrusive on the liberties of persons to act as they please. It seems useful to distinguish these two elements in the argument. I may summarize them by stating that Musgrave is both more *optimistic* about the workings of democratic politics than I am, which is the first difference noted above, and more *paternalistic* than I am, the second difference noted. Although conceptually distinct, these two basic differences cannot be totally separated in their implications. Both reasons combine to make Musgrave's normatively idealized public sector larger than my own.

I am reminded of the familiar situation where two persons see the bottle of wine, the first of whom defines the bottle to be half-full, while the second of whom says it is half-empty. Both Musgrave and I may agree that the state, inclusively defined, is a complex set of institutional arrangements that can accomplish much that is "good," as evaluated by members of the political community, but that the state can also exert a negative impact—that is, can do much that is "bad"—again as evaluated by persons who are participants in the whole collective enterprise. My differences with Musgrave can be summarized along a unidimensional spectrum, with neither of us located at the extremes. He places considerably more relative weight on the "good" that collective action can do, whereas I place more relative weight on the "bad" that unconstrained collective action might do.

Given our differences in the evaluations of the efficacy of political or collective action, it follows that we may also differ as to the efficacy and desirability of constitutional constraints that might be imposed on the authority of governments. By common presupposition, we agree that constraints do, indeed, constrain or limit actions, and, in so doing, both "good" and "bad" actions may be forestalled. My self-assigned task in this lecture is to lay out the positive argument in support of constitutional constraints on the exercise of political authority by governments as carried out in what we may call "ordinary politics," reflected in the operation of elected parliamentary or legislative majorities.

One further point should be made in this introduction. I have discussed the basic argument here in many different settings over the course of several decades. I have always been reluctant to use material prepared for earlier occasions. This lecture is new in the sense that I have rewritten familiar stuff from the 1998 perspective. But I make no claim to any newfound originality here. In support for rehashing old arguments, I can only cite Herbert Spenser who, in the preface to his book *The Data of Ethics*, stated that "only by varied reiteration can alien conceptions be forced on reluctant minds." Perhaps this 1998 reiteration will be sufficiently varied to achieve the purpose.

II We Are All Constitutionalists

Let me first clear common ground by suggesting that *some* constraints on the exercise of political authority are considered by almost everyone to be essential for a functioning social order; there can be no disagreement between the two of us on this point. The basic constitutional constraints that require agents for the collectivity to submit themselves to regular elections and to possible replacement in office, that allow all citizens to hold the voting franchise with equal weights assigned to each, that place few limits on eligibility for political office, that specify voting rules both for the election of representatives and for decision making in legislative assemblies, that place restrictions on the assigned authority of nonelected bureaucrats and judges—there is little or no quarrel or dispute concerning the necessary presence of this set of limits on politics.

The issues that may provoke dispute arise when we introduce constraints on political authority that go beyond these standard and agreed-on limits, beyond what we may here call "electoral constraints," which, at base, insure the members of the polity that they possess the residual opportunity to "throw the rascals out" but do little to restrict directly what elected agents may do so long as the electoral rules are respected.

In other, and earlier, elaborations of the argument developed in this lecture, I have traced some of the history and I have often referred to the "electoral fallacy" that invaded conventional discourse about politics, especially during the nineteenth and twentieth centuries. In earlier periods, when governments were organized nondemocratically, as monarchies or aristocracies, there was a generalized recognition of the desirability of imposing constraints on what governments could do. Indeed, modern parliamentary regimes emerged in the long struggle to limit the powers of the monarch and, notably, the power to tax.

As effective authority was shifted from the monarch to the legislative assembly, however, the potential for electoral checks came to be treated as sufficient. Why impose limits on authority, as such, so long as governments are made up of elected representatives, subject to electoral rejection and removal by the citizenry? I have called the inferred answer to this question fallacious in the sense that legislative assemblies no less than, and perhaps even more than, nonelected rulers may require constraints that place boundaries on acceptable actions. Indeed, claims of electoral legitimacy may often be used as excuses for the extension of political authority beyond any limits that may ultimately be adjudged in the interests of the citizenry generally.

III The Logic of Limits

Why should any constraints be placed on the exercise of political authority by duly elected governments so long as action is taken within established procedures? To make the argument for constitutional constraints, it is necessary, first of all, to derive the elementary logic of limits or constraints on the exercise of free or voluntary choice, whether at the level of an individual or a collectivity.

As a preliminary point, we should note that economists, in their disciplinary mindset, may be quite uncomfortable when confronted with analyses that involves choices among constraints. Economists spend most of their intellectual energies analyzing models in which actors are postulated to be choosing among options open to them within the set of constraints that they confront, constraints that are exogenous to the behavior that is examined. Within this familiar setting, the solution to the maximizing exercise is conceptually straightforward once the maximand is defined. The economists' natural query becomes: Why should anyone ever choose to constrain the choice set? Choices among constraints themselves become foreign territory for the ordinary practicing professional.

An elementary, and in part empirical, understanding of the logic of limits may be gained by a cursory examination of the research program that involves choice behavior in situations where persons voluntarily impose restrictions on their own private actions. Persons do adopt rules that they intend to be binding, rules that are aimed to prevent specific actions. They adopt and abide by dietary plans; they purchase stop-smoking aids; they join Alcoholics Anonymous; they do not go to Las Vegas. In each case, and others, they are taking action that is designed to restrict choices that they consider to have undesirable consequences but that will be tempting in the immediate context. The example from classical mythology is Ulysses, who directed his oarsmen to tie him to the mast and to remain deaf to his entreaties as the ship sails past the sirens' shore (Elster 1979).

The ongoing research program here might be described under the rubric of "individual constitutional rules." It is clear, however, that any logic of limits on collective action is categorically different from that which applies only to individual choice behavior. For by far the greater part of ordinary day-to-day behavior, persons presumably prefer to leave their options open, to remain free to choose as the occasion dictates, to trust in their own judgment. In other words, the deliberate constraints mentioned in the examples above are exceptions to the norm. The "realm of rules" may be relatively small. The individual does not really fear the consequences of her free choices.

The "reason of rules" (Brennan and Buchanan 1985) is quite different when we shift attention from individual to collective action. In the latter, persons may well prefer to impose prior limits on possible actions, not in order to restrict their own behavior but to restrict the behavior of others whose actions may impose net costs in the context of political interaction. That is to say, the individual may prefer to impose specific limits on collective action even if, in some private capacity, no self-imposed rules would be chosen.

The individual who chooses to support, at some constitutional stage of deliberation, constraints on ordinary political actions will, of course, recognize that any such constraints will narrow the range of possible collective outcomes, sometimes to the detriment of her own interests. But the possible damages to one's own interests, which enter as anticipated costs of the constraints, may be judged to be lower than the benefits expected to be secured by the limits on the potentially damaging behavior of others, as implemented through collective actions.

IV The Natural Discrimination of Majority Rule

At this point, a critic might ask why any individual, as a member of a political community, might fear that her interests would be harmed by collective actions taken by duly elected agents delegated to govern. The response is straightforward. As they must operate, governmental agents can, at best, represent the interests of the members of the coalition whose support placed them in positions of authority. In the absence of nonelectoral constraints, those agents will, naturally, discriminate in favor of their supporters and against those who supported others. Nondiscriminatory action will be dominated by discriminatory action and for whomever makes up the relevant ruling coalition. (See Buchanan 1998 for the basic analysis.) The individual will anticipate differentially advantageous collective treatment when she succeeds in becoming a member of a majority coalition, but she must also anticipate differentially disadvantageous collective treatment when she is placed in a minority.

The operation of majoritarian political institutions may be illustrated through the use of highly stylized and simplified models. Suppose that there are only three persons (or groups of like persons) in the political unit, which operates through simple majority voting rules. Suppose, first, that there is known to exist a project that will yield commonly shared benefits (a genuine public good in the conventional sense) in the amount of \$4 per person. The project can be undertaken for a total outlay of \$9. The aggregate "social" benefits are \$3. But note that neither a single person nor any group of two persons will find it worthwhile to finance the project unless exclusion is possible at low cost. Collective action by the group organized collectively is required.

One outcome or solution is that shown as Alternative I in table 1 below, in which the commonly shared good is financed by equal taxes imposed on all beneficiaries. Each of the three persons shares equally in the net value that the project generates. There is no discrimination.

But why should the majority coalition that finds itself in political authority choose the outcome depicted as Alternative I? If the majority is, say, *AB*, why would this majority not finance the project by imposing all of the tax costs on *C*,

Table 1

	Person	Benefit Value	Tax	Net Value
	A	4	3	+1
Alternative I	B	4	3	+1
	C	4	3	+1
	A	4	0	4
Alternative II	B	4	0	4
	C	4	9	−5
	A	4	0	4
Alternative III	B	4	0	4
	C	4	15	−11
	A	4.5	0	4.5
Alternative IV	B	4.5	0	4.5
	C	0	9	−9

thereby generating the outcome shown as Alternative II in table 1? This solution clearly dominates that in Alternative I for all members of the majority coalition, and a similar result holds for any other possible majority. An outcome analogous to that in II will dominate I for any majority.

Note that, as illustrated here, the net social value remains at $3 in both of the outcomes depicted. But the distribution of this net value necessarily reflects majoritarian discrimination. Note also that the project used in this simple model is, in itself, economically efficient, in the sense that aggregate benefits exceed total costs. This result is, however, an artifact produced arbitrarily by the postulated arithmetic. There is no insurance that majoritarian politics will always choose to undertake only efficient projects. Consider Alternative III in table 1, in which the aggregate benefit from the commonly shared good remains at $12 , as before. But assume that the total costs sum to say, $15. If the AB majority can impose the full costs on C, their own gain remains at $4 per person, as in Alternative II. But the negative value or damage imposed on C more than offsets the gains to members of the majority.

To this point, I have implicitly assumed that majoritarian collective action is restricted to the financing of commonly shared, nonpartitionable goods and services. If this assumption is dropped, and collective actions extended to allow for direct redistributive transfers between members of majority and minority coalitions, it becomes clear that any majority may prefer to initiate direct transfers than to seek gains indirectly through public goods financing. Suppose, rather than finance the project depicted in Alternative I, the AB majority could simply levy the tax of $9 on C and transfer the proceeds to themselves, symmetrically shared. This generates the outcome shown in table 1 as Alternative IV, which dominates that in I, II, or III for members of the majority coalition. If such direct fiscal transfers are possible, no inefficient project will be financed, and genuinely efficient public-goods projects will be approved only if the aggregate benefits, in the limiting case, are more than double the total costs.[2] The essential logic of unconstrained majority rule for collective decision making implies both that discrimination between majority and minority interests will take place and that there will be a budgetary allocation bias against commonly shared collective consumption goods in favor of direct transfers or targeted programs.

So far, so good. But even if this central logic is accepted, critics may suggest that I have not yet fully established the case for the imposition of constitutional constraints on the exercise of political authority by majoritarian coalitions. A further step in the analysis is required. If all members of the inclusive political constituency retain an equal chance of securing membership in winning majority coalitions, and if we ignore discounting, the expected value of collective action could possibly remain the same whether or not the effective majority coalition is constitutionally limited. In the simple illustrative example above, the net "social" values of the project under Alternative I and Alternative II are equal; expected values are the same. And, if direct transfers are allowed, this conclusion also may be extended.

Three separate difficulties exist with any claim that expected values remain the same with and without anticipated majoritarian discrimination. First, and as the

---

2. In a polity with n members, assume that financing a commonly, and equally, shared public good yields aggregate benefits B, or B/n per person at an aggregate cost of C. By comparison, for the same outlay, C, direct fiscal transfers per member of the majority can be implemented in the amount of $C/(n/2+1)$. Hence the public goods alternative will be viable only if $B > 2C$, in the limit.

analysis above indicated, some projects that yield negative aggregate value, in net, may be financed if direct transfers are not permissible, and, if such transfers are permissible, some projects that yield positive net value will not be undertaken. Hence, expected values will not be the same under nonconstrained and constrained majoritarian politics. Second, even if this argument is ignored, the presence of risk averseness will dictate the relative superiority of an institutional setting with less rather than more discriminatory collective action. Third, and important, there will be costs involved in the rotation of discriminatory majoritarian coalitions over and beyond those that stem from divergencies among tax prices and benefits flows. In the unconstrained setting, there are clear advantages to be secured from membership in dominant majority coalitions, along with disadvantages from being left in an exploited minority. The differentials between positions here will attract investment in efforts to insure majority membership. Rent seeking may be quite large here, and this, in itself, uses up resources that might otherwise be put to value producing employment (see Buchanan 1995). If it is acknowledged that such rent-seeking outlays will be reduced, perhaps substantially, in the presence of constitutional constraints, the expected value of membership in the collectivity will be larger for this reason alone.

V Procedural and Domain Constraints on Political Authority

What form should constraints on the authority of duly elected governments take? As I suggested in my introductory lecture, there are two conceptually separate forms or types of constraints that may be identified. And, in my own analysis as well as advocacy, I have variously been in both camps, so to speak. We may label these forms as impacting on rules for reaching collective decisions (hence, *procedural* in nature) or on the set of permissible outcomes or solutions that may be allowed under any agreed-on procedures (hence, *domain* restricting in nature).

Knut Wicksell's (1896) emphasis was on rules, and he suggested that a change from majority voting in legislative or parliamentary assemblies toward more inclusive requirements (in the limit, unanimity) would tend to increase prospects that collective action would, in net, be efficiency enhancing rather than efficiency reducing. The simple numerical examples introduced earlier, and summarized in figure 1, can illustrate the thrust of Wicksell's proposition. Note that the replacement of simple majority rule by the unanimity rule would, in the setting of the examples, limit or restrict the collective outcomes to that designated as Alternative I. Only efficiency-enhancing projects would be selected, since efficiency is itself defined by the evaluations of persons and no person will vote for a project that yields negative benefits. Discrimination against minority members would not be possible.

Again, as noted in my introductory lecture, in *The Calculus of Consent* (Buchanan and Tullock 1962) Gordon Tullock and I were working within the Wicksellian paradigm, and that book's argument may be summarized as a plea for replacing majority rule by more inclusive rules, at least for critically important collective actions. Over the four decades since that work, however, I have been forced, reluctantly, to acknowledge the normative strength that majority rule has in public attitudes, involving the equation of majoritarianism with democracy itself, at least in some deep evaluative sense. If, then, we are forced to abandon the Wicksellian avenue for constitutional reform, and to accept that legislative assemblies are likely to continue to operate by majority rule, however this rule may be institutionally tempered in practice, we are left with possible limits on the domain of permissible outcomes as the only means of constraining political discrimination.

As I also noted in my introductory lecture, my book, with Roger Congleton, entitled *Politics by Principle, Not Interest* (Buchanan and Congleton 1998), with the subtitle *Toward Nondiscriminatory Democracy,* develops the analysis of such domain constraints in some detail. Again, I can resort to the simple numerical example. Suppose that majority rule remains in place, but now suppose that a constitutional constraint dictates that collective action must be *nondiscriminatory* as it affects all persons in the polity. Note that, in this setting, the *AB* majority coalition (or any other) could only choose the first option, Alternative I, which does provide benefits and exacts taxes generally rather than in a discriminatory fashion. The alternative outcomes depicted as II, III, and IV will remain out-of-bounds under such a generality constraint.

In the highly abstracted models used here, we may also note that the replacement of majority rule by the unanimity rule, on the one hand, and the imposition of the generality constraint, on the other, would yield identical results. Both of these quite distinct constitutional changes will insure that only the first alternative, I, emerges as the collective action. Implicit in the numerical example, however, is the assumption that the participants are equal, both in their evaluations of the commonly shared good, and in their capacities to pay taxes for the financing of this good. If this assumption of equality is dropped, in either or both of the relevant dimensions here, there will be differences in patterns of collective outcomes generated under the two separate forms of constraint, those that act to modify procedures for reaching decisions and those that restrict the domain.

I cannot in this lecture, which must remain a summary treatment, elaborate on the differences between the operation of these two forms of constraint in detail, even if analysis is restricted to the use of highly stylized models. I can only, once again, make reference to our 1998 book. Nonetheless, I can try here to sketch out some of the main features in a comparative framework. Any change in the rules for reaching collective decisions in the direction of greater inclusivity, or greater consensus, must reduce the relative size of the group that may be differentially damaged through collective action. But inclusivity, as such, does not prevent adjustments that allow differential matchings of benefits and burdens. Targeted spending, if matched by comparably targeted taxation, may pass muster under supramajority rules. Discrimination on either the spending or taxing side of the fiscal account may remain possible, even in the supramajoritarian setting; what is not possible is discriminatory exploitation as measured in the net operations of the two sides of the account.

The situation under the domain constraint of generality becomes quite different. Here, majority rule will tend to generate outcomes that are those preferred by the median voter. But some voters, or groups, may find majoritarian outcomes less preferred than others that might also meet the generality requirement, including maintenance of the status quo ante.[3] On the other hand, the generality constraint does

3. Under standard assumptions about convexities in individual preference orderings, majority voting will not generate the familiar cycles if the alternatives for choice are restricted to those that satisfy the generality constraint. Geometrically, we may think of these alternatives as those that lie

insure that collective action remain genuinely "public" in the sense that benefits must be equally available to all participants (even if not required by the technology of production and delivery) and that taxes be imposed on established criteria of generality. The degree of explicit minority exploitation is severely limited. What the generality constraint eliminates are specifically targeted benefits (and transfers) and specifically targeted taxation. The "natural" discriminatory features of majority rule are not allowed to operate, although potentially efficiency-enhancing two-sided discrimination is also ruled out-of-bounds.

VI Fiscal Redistribution and Constitutional Constraints

The difference in effects of these two forms of constitutional constraints on political authority emerges perhaps most clearly when we examine the prospects for redistributive action by the collectivity. If majority rule is replaced by the unanimity rule, in actuality or in some approximation through supramajority requirements, the redistribution of incomes or wealth through the auspices of the collectivity must be severely limited. Under unanimity, only on agreement among all members of the polity can transfers to selected persons be implemented. Some fiscal redistribution toward the poor may find general support; in other words, some Pareto-superior redistribution may take place, even under highly inclusive procedural rules. Such redistribution would be much less than might take place under unconstrained majority rules. But whether or not the poor, as a group, would necessarily be made better off in the uncon-

---

along the diagonal within the n-dimensional "cube," where the separate dimensions measure the inputs of different persons toward the financing of the commonly shared good.

strained setting might be questioned. In any distributional context, majority rule must generate the familiar cycles, and there is no assurance that those persons and groups most in need of fiscal support would fare well in the cyclical rotation.

By contrast with the procedural requirement that operates on the inclusivity of the voting rule, a generality constraint, applied to the domain of outcomes for collective action, may be interpreted to allow for considerable redistributive activity, under some definitions of the generality criterion. As already noted, collective outlay would be restricted to the financing of genuinely public goods made available to all persons or groups within the polity, or, if partitionable goods (including cash transfers) were financed, these would have to be offered in equal amounts to all persons. On the outlay side, a scheme of equal-per-head payments, or demogrants, would surely meet most generality norms.

On the taxing side of the account, the generality criterion raises more difficult questions of definition. Strictly interpreted, equal-per-head taxes would qualify, but any such scheme would, of course, prevent any and all net redistribution. A more plausible interpretation of the generality criterion here would be the requirement that taxes be imposed *generally* on a well-defined base that relates to individual taxpayer capacity, on traditional ability-to-pay measures. But, importantly, the generality principle could allow for no exemptions, deductions, credits, exclusions for any persons or groups.

A flat rate or proportional tax levied on *all* income (the scheme that Luigi Einaudi proposed for many years) with transfers in the form of equal-per-head demogrants would seem to meet most definitions of the generality norm. Note that such a set of operative constraints would possibly allow for considerable net fiscal redistribution, as to be settled by the median voters in the majoritarian process. Clearly, those with below-median incomes would prefer a high-tax, high-demogrant alternative, whereas those with above-median incomes would prefer a low-tax, low-demogrant alternative. But, in one sense, the political dialogue would be concerned with the level of *generalized* redistribution to be implemented through the fiscal structure, rather than with the "deservingness" or "nondeservingness" of this or that particularly identified group of potential recipients or potential taxpayers. Such a system would act to eliminate the emergence of what Anthony de Jasay has called "the churning state" (de Jasay 1985). There would be no shifting back and forth among coalitions of shifting groups of differentially benefited and differentially damaged sets of persons. Furthermore, significant social losses would be forestalled by the elimination of incentives for investment in efforts to secure differentially favorable or to avoid differentially unfavorable fiscal treatment.

Under a flat-rate proportional income tax, without exemptions, exclusions, credits, or deductions, along with equal-per-head demogrants, there might still remain a bias in overall budgetary allocation toward transfers as opposed to the financing of efficiency-enhancing public goods, but the elimination of fiscal targeting, as dictated by any type of generality constraint, would surely restore much public respect for modern democratic processes that seems to have been lost over this century.

Less inclusive schemes of fiscal redistribution may possibly qualify as quasi-general, with the criterion being that eligibility for receipt of transfers cannot be determined

either by adjustments in private behavior or by political
affiliation. Transfers to the old (everyone who lives becomes
old) at least partially meet this requirement.

VII Toward Institutional Reality

I have discussed the efficacy of possible constitutional constraints on the exercise of political authority, constraints that
are beyond those embodied in the familiar set of electoral
rules. I have presented the argument for such additional
constraints through the use of highly simplified analytical
models. I propose, in the last part of my lecture, to bring the
discussion down to earth, at least in some part, and to try
to relate the analysis to the modern institutional reality of
Western democracies.

I have discussed constitutional constraints within a dual
classification: those that might operate on rules or procedures for reaching collective choices and those that might
operate directly on the set of outcomes or positions that may
be generated whatever the rules of decision. The first point
to be made, as we try to relate the analysis to reality, is to
suggest that both sets of constraints do indeed exist in modern democratic politics and that both sets do act to reduce,
and perhaps very substantially, the degree, range, and extent
of possible political discrimination and, by inference, the
social wastage of resources reflected in rent-seeking investments. In other words, as presented here, the simple analytical models tend to exaggerate the effects of what I have
called the "natural" discrimination inherent in majoritarianism, as such.

First, consider procedures or rules. Governmental actions
are not, in fact, made as a result of processes that involve
nothing more than up-and-down majority voting in legisla-

tive assemblies. In all structures, collective actions finally emerge from a complex institutional setting that might well be best modeled in a supramajoritarian rather than a majoritarian framework. The United States offers an example. With a two-house legislature, an executive veto, and independent judicial review, any collective action presumably requires the equivalent of considerably more than majority support. European parliamentary structures in which collective decisions are made, effectively, by governments organized by political parties, singly or in coalitions, more closely resemble the textbook models of majority rule. But, even here, actions normally command more than bare majority approval.

On the other hand, when we shift attention to domain considerations, and particularly as we focus attention on the presence or absence of some generality norm, the American structure seems more vulnerable to criticism along the lines of the simple analysis sketched out earlier. Collective action that emerges may represent a coalition of particular interests, as embodied in exchanges of support among a set of pressure or interest groups, with little or no coherence or objective beyond the single issue defined by the action. The apparent targeting in both the spending and taxing sides of budgets may reflect little more than some ultimate and quite arbitrary classification or dividing line between successful and unsuccessful rent seekers.

In both European and American systems, however, the effective constitutional embodiment of elements of the rule of law operates to prevent blatant political discrimination along many dimensions. Persons and groups cannot be arbitrarily targeted either for especially onerous tax treatment or for receipt of special benefits. Differentially high rates of tax levied on persons strictly because of race, ethnicity, religion, gender, or political history and affiliation would not be deemed constitutionally permissible by the courts. Differentially favorable spending programs are held to less rigorous generalization standards, although some standards nonetheless apply, even here. At least lip service is paid to the satisfaction of "public interest" classifications.

When the account is assessed overall, however, much arbitrary political discrimination does take place within currently applicable constitutional limits. Governments, or dominating majority coalitions, may single out particular groups for either differential rewards or punishments, so long as the discrimination does not break down along lines like those listed above. Specific industries, professions, occupations, consumers, investors, personal practices, locational preferences—these and other groups may be made net beneficiaries or net losers in the churning activity of the coalitions that describes modern democratic politics. To me, it would be difficult to argue that operative constraints, as they now exist, on majoritarian processes are, somehow, optimal, and, therefore, not subjected to challenge with some objective of reform. The challenge remains one of adjusting the institutions of politics so as to insure that the public economy remains efficiency enhancing rather than efficiency reducing, and, importantly, that these institutions be seen as such by participants in the inclusive collective enterprise.

Note that my classification of the challenge as institutional rather than behavioral incorporates my presumption that persons in their roles as "public choosers," whether as constituency members or as political agents, retain essentially the same behavioral characteristics that they exhibit in their nonpublic roles, as participants in ordinary private pursuits. This presumption yields the straightforward prediction that persons, singly or in groups, will seek to further their own interests as they participate in the public and in the private economy. Politicians and bureaucrats do not become saints when they assume agency roles, nor would they survive long electorally if they did so.

I recognize, of course, that there are institutional feedbacks that may affect behavior and make for relevant differences between the two sectors. Precisely because persons recognize that they must choose for others as well as for themselves in collective decision settings, persons may incorporate some of the spillover effects of their own choices into their subjective evaluations of collective choice alternatives. Just as the externality-characterized "market failures," familiar from Pigovian welfare economics, may be less damaging than they seem to be from the stylized models due to possible subjective internalization (Buchanan 1969), so the externality-characterized "political failures" may be less efficiency reducing than they seem to be in the stylized models developed earlier in this lecture. This qualification does not, however, undermine the essential logic of the analytical construction.

Postscript: Political Exit

In deference to our mutually agreed-on and assigned subject matter for session 4, which is federalism, I have deliberately based the whole discussion and analysis of this lecture in the implicit assumption that the questions of possible constitutional constraints on political authority arise in settings where the costs of exit from the political community are prohibitively high. To the extent that this assumption is descriptive of political and economic reality, individuals, singly or in groups, are subject to political discrimination under majoritarian governance. By contrast, to the extent that costs of exit are low, marketlike exit options act to limit, and perhaps severely, any potential for fiscal exploitation. All reductions in the costs of exit therefore lessen any need for reforms aimed at modifying majoritarian procedures or at placing more restricted boundaries on permissible sets of political outcomes.

3.2 Response

Richard A. Musgrave

I can readily agree with Professor Buchanan's view of the state as a complex institution, which can accomplish much that is good as well as much that is bad, and I am pleased to have him say so. We are not here to discuss the comparative merits of anarchy and totalitarianism. Government is needed and the question is what it should and should not do. I also agree that, measured on a unidimensional scale, my position is closer to the good and his to the bad end and that therefore I would restrain government less than he would. I agree but am not quite comfortable with that last formulation and would amend it slightly.

I Subjects of Restraint

To ask by how much the state should be restrained—the perspective set in the title to the paper—leaves the state as a defendant who must prove his innocence. This overlooks that it is not only the state whose actions need be restrained. In order to emerge from the Hobbesian jungle, social coexistence also requires restraints on what individuals are free to do. To impose such restraints, collective action by the democratic state is needed. It is thus the proper mix of restraints, imposed on collective and individual actions, respectively, that matters; and it is that mix that should be written into our scale, and not restraint on state action only. Thereby, the lecture's unidimensional scale, adequate to measure temperature but not issues in social science, has to be replaced by a multidimensional perspective.

Professor Buchanan begins where this basic bundle of restraints has already been decided upon in favor of the democratic state, with its standard institutions. Citizens have equal voting rights, agents of the state must stand for election and reelection, the role of legislative assemblies has been established, and so forth. He suggests that these constraints on the exercise of political authority (I would prefer to say "these measures to exercise and restrain political authority") are held essential for a functioning social order by almost everyone, and that there can be no disagreement between us on that point. Disputes arise only, so he argues, when we consider what further restraints on political authority should be imposed or, as I prefer to put it, what further restraints and obligations should be needed.

Given that common foundation, search for the proper size of budgets might involve two further directions of inquiry. The first looks at the scale of collective action as determined by a set of "objective" circumstances, consumer preferences, resources, and technology—that is, by how large is the commons, how prevailing are externalities, what is the shape of the community's social welfare function, and what does all this tell us about the "proper" size of the budget. This was the direction that I took in yesterday's lecture. Professor Buchanan now turns to a second direction, that is, the decision-making process that underlies collective action, and especially to the central issue of choice by voting. Other old friends of his Leviathan model, such as self-aggrandizing governmental agents and fiscal illusion, are set aside (I take it, only for the time being), and I will do so as well (R. A. Musgrave 1981a).

II Model '98

Professor Buchanan begins with the familiar proposition that majority rule is not an optimal arrangement, whether in the context of positive-sum games such as the provision of public goods or in zero-sum games such as transfers. Discrimination, rent seeking, and excessive budgets are said to result. The complaint is familiar and the question is what to do about it.

The remedy, offered in the Buchanan-Tullock epic of 1962, was to move from simple majority to unanimity or unanimity qualified by allowance for transaction costs. Buchanan Model '98 breaks with that Wicksellian faith. "I have been forced," so we are now told, "reluctantly to acknowledge the normative strength that majority rule has in public attitudes, involving the equation of majoritarianism with democracy itself, at least in some deep evaluative sense." I am not sure whether I can detect a measure of approval of that popular wisdom and a crack in Professor Buchanan's philosophical armor, or only a political judgment that, foolish as people are, majority rule is here to stay. Perhaps he will tell us.

Given that concession, but distrusting the outcome, Professor Buchanan then clips its wings by superimposing what he calls a "domain" of nondiscrimination. Majoritarian decisionmaking must be limited to propositions that, when enacted, have outcomes that are nondiscriminatory. Thereby, he hopes to restrict rent seeking and reduce the size of the budget. At the more philosophical level, a fundamental shift in methodology has occurred. The conservative dictum that what matters is rules, not outcomes (a position that I used to associate with him) is discarded. Astride Model '98, he now joins our band of outcome-oriented reformers.

Then there is a third feature of the new model. In the 1962 version, the choice process and voting rules were discussed only in relation to the positive-sum game (I dislike that playful term—public policy is not a sandbox!) of providing for public goods. Model '62, as I recall, took the just state of distribution as predetermined at an early stage of constitution-making. Majoritarian choices later on could have distributional effects, but distributional change itself was not a legitimate policy goal. This is no longer the case with Model '98. Here distributional measures *are* allowed for, provided only that they respect the impartiality domain. A further crack in the armor, so it seems, but to me it is another attractive feature of the new model.

III In Defense of the Majority Rule

When the lecture refers to "the normative strength which majority rule has in public attitudes," let me reveal myself as a member of that public and suggest that its position is not without reason. If we accept the democratic premise that each vote is to carry equal weight, is there no prima facie case for a solution that balances the number of winners against that of losers, with a resolution to pass only if there are more winners? This, to be sure, disregards differences in the intensity by which positions are held and presumes additivity, but much of that is implied already in the premise of equal weights. When compared with a setting that grants veto or enactment rights to a small minority, the majority rule becomes a move toward, not a rejection of, the Wicksellian solution.

While offering this common sense support for majority rule, I do not wish to overlook its imperfections, such as cycling, logrolling, agenda manipulation, and so forth. Nor do I wish to exclude that other but related arrangements, such as point voting, may not prove superior in some settings or that more sophisticated approaches aimed at preference revelation, such as the Clark tax, are not worth considering. My point merely is that simple majority rule has its rationale and is not quite as bad as Professor Buchanan suggests.

IV Cohesiveness and the Role of Coalitions

Much depends on the cohesiveness of society and the extent to which its preferences tend to converge or to differ. The median voter model is not only a matter of textbook convenience but becomes operational where preferences are single peaked and acceptable where departure from the mean is not too diverse. As applied to single issues, such should be the prevailing case if society is to function at all.

Majority rule becomes more troublesome where coalitions are formed to bundle diverse issues. Preferences regarding the size of highway or school budgets may well be bunched and single peaked, but preferences regarding the allocation of budgetary resources between the two may not. Thus coalitions are formed and agendas are set, which complicate the outcome of majority rule. Such is especially the case where fiscal issues are combined with a wide variety of other concerns. Smokers without cars may combine with non-smokers who drive, trading support for highways for support against smoking restrictions. Positions on gun control, abortion, fox hunting, or Saturday shopping may be paired with positions on defense budgets or welfare. Nevertheless, the outcome of majority rule is not as chaotic and destructive as the paper seems to suggest, or as theoretical analysis may lead one to expect. Thus even Dennis Mueller is led to wonder why the system is as stable as it is (1989, 49).

To explain why, I suggest more attention needs to be paid to how and why preference groups and coalitions are formed, and what are the circumstances that make them coalesce or diverge. This need, I think, is not met by modeling choice behavior of existing agents (Professor Buchanan's "prevailing coalitions ") in the spirit of economic microtheory. Rather, and in line with what I said in my first paper, public-choice scholars should take a look at authors such as Marx, Weber, and Schumpeter to explore how society functions and how coalitions come to prevail. It is individuals who matter in the end, but it is groups of individuals who act and determine outcomes in a democratic society. There are, of course, authors such as Mancur Olson who recognized this and whose recent untimely death should be noted here, but he has been an exception to the rule among public choice scholars.

V Majoritarian Rule and Discrimination

Dissatisfaction with majority rule in Buchanan's Model '62 had focused on the tendency of coalition-based logrolling to generate excessive budgets. Extending Tullock's classic access roads case (1959), coalitions will support their respective special interest projects while using broad-based finance to which others must contribute. Perhaps so, but vote trading may also lead to deficient as well as excessive budgets, and so may side payments (Mueller 1989, 84). As with the median voter model, there is no general presumption that voting imperfections must exaggerate budget size. The opposite may also occur.

In today's lecture, Professor Buchanan considers the effect of vote trading on the provision of commonly beneficial or pure public goods. He shows how coalitions may agree to shift the burden to the minority by raising its tax share and increasing the budget at their cost. Voting themselves transfer payments, they may drive out public goods.

Discrimination results, I agree, because pursuit of redistributional gains is mixed in with the provision of public goods. True enough, but it does not follow that redistributional policies have no place in the budget. What follows is that they should be conducted separately, and not mixed in. This, of course, was precisely what I had in mind when, following Wicksell, I asked for separation of the allocation and distribution branches (R. A. Musgrave 1959). I fear that Professor Buchanan's prescription fails to do so. By extending his domain of nondiscrimination over the entire budget, distribution and allocation branches alike, he also limits the scope for pursuing distributional objectives on their own terms, or indeed precludes such goals. I am not sure, therefore, that I can welcome him as a member of my club.

Under Professor Buchanan's plan, a proportional income tax would be used to finance public goods, supplemented by a similarly financed demogrant to implement redistribution. It is not made clear, however, whether the vote would be on the budget as a whole, or whether the levels of public goods and their finance would be set separately from the level of the demogrant and its finance. The distinction is crucial since the two issues differ. The median voter on the level of public services may well differ from that on the

demogrant. To avoid distortions, separation of the two issues is crucial. Einaudi and Wicksell cannot be embraced at
the same time.

I also wonder how far the Buchanan plan would go in
keeping coalitions from exploiting the nonmember minority.
Discrimination can take two forms. One case, shown in the
table, involves putting the tax burden on the minority, which
will suffer even if its preferences for public goods are similar
to those of the coalition. Here a uniform tax rule will help.
But the uniform tax remedy does not work for a second case
where preferences differ, as initially featured in Tullock's
access roads case. There the coalition may vote in projects
that give no benefits to the minority that must contribute,
causing discrimination even if the tax is uniform. This, I
think, is the much more important case. Even though the
income tax is not wholly uniform, it is fairly so. Discrimination via generally financed special-interest pork barrel legislation, however, is open-ended.

Buchanan's rule of generality should therefore be required
to hold at the expenditure side as well. But how is this to
be done? Voting on specified tax-expenditure bundles in the
aggregate would hamstring coalitions, but who is to decide
how these bundles are to be composed? Or, should each
project and its finance be voted upon separately, as I have
suggested, rather than in aggregate budget bills (R. A. Musgrave 1981c)? Does the quest for nondiscrimination in the
end reduce to benefit taxation? I can only pose these queries
here, but it seems evident that this is where the real problem
lies and I suggest that it be dealt with in the Buchanan Model
2000.

I also have a problem with addressing redistribution via
a proportional tax-financed demogrant. This is similar in
outcome to a declining rate of income subsidy when moving
from the bottom up toward the middle of the income scale,

followed by a slowly rising rate of tax, approaching a limit set by the subsidy cost as a percent of the available tax base. The more the lower end is to be raised, the larger will be the required transfer of funds and the resulting level of fiscal churning. This approach, moreover, precludes the application of progressive taxation over the middle-upper and upper end of the income scale, leaving the top rate substantially below what it would be under even a moderate degree of progression in bracket rates. This would be a high price to pay, particularly in the United States where the income share of the top range is so inordinately high. As with the flat tax plans now proposed in the United States, what seems such a simple and attractive scheme soon becomes a device to protect the wealthy. I do not mean to attribute this motivation to Professor Buchanan, having thought of him as a Rawlsian, but I would like to hear him respond to that point.

At the cost of trespassing into our final topic, I would also question the use of the demogrant as a way to deal with the poor. Welfare policy, as I have argued in an earlier discussion with him, cannot be wholly general and must be selective. A welfare scheme that pays equal benefits to everyone either fails to meet the needs at the bottom or, if adequate, calls for very large budgets. Moreover, depending on the needs that have to be met—old age, health, incapacity, and so forth—different remedies are called for and cannot be equalized by a uniform formula of support. Like it or not, redistribution by its very nature must differentiate between donors and donees. Targeted differentiation, as an appropriate policy goal, must be distinguished from wanton discrimination, be it unequal treatment of equals in taxation (with which our band of tax reformers has battled for over five decades) or arbitrary exclusion of particular groups from expenditure benefits.

3.3   Discussion

Sinn: Now we have questions from the floor. Please.

Alan Williams, University of York: James Buchanan, on Monday I teased you a little by suggesting that deep down you are a rule utilitarian, and you said then that you believed in rules, but there was no way you could be regarded as utilitarian, although you were a consequentialist. In the light of what you said today, I see why you made that distinction. Your domain restriction concept is in the realm of consequences, but presumably the maximand in that area of consequences is not the maximization of individual utilities, otherwise, you would be back being a utilitarian again. But I am a little puzzled about what the maximand now is. From earlier writings of yours, one might suppose that the maximand is some notion of liberty, but you are also obviously greatly interested in some kinds of equality of treatment between individuals, so there could actually be two broad ideological strands in this area of consequences. One is liberty, the other would be equality, in which case you have to think about trade-offs. If so, it may turn out that the only difference between you and Richard Musgrave is how much weight you each give to liberty as opposed to equality. So there appears to be a very simple solution: it is all about trade-offs and the social welfare function. The alternative interpretation, which comes closer to conventional economic thinking, is that what is in the domain of your maximand is equity and efficiency, which isn't quite the same thing as equality and efficiency, because there are many other notions of equity besides the egalitarian notions, and efficiency would then be some kind of Pareto efficiency. Now if those are the elements that you see as being in the domain of your consequences, when you are thinking about domain restrictions, then the idea of discrimination or nondiscrimination rather falls away, because whether the discriminatory rules are acceptable or not would have to depend upon their impact upon your efficiency or equity objectives. So some discriminations will be efficient, some will be inefficient; some discriminations will be fair, and some will be unfair. The generality rule that you proposed then becomes a means to achieve these higher-level objectives. I wonder whether this interpretation of your views is acceptable to you or not. If it is acceptable, I think I am with you one hundred percent, except that my trade offs in the social welfare function will be a little different from yours.

Peter Bernholz, University of Basel: Well, I have to say there is no social welfare function. But apart from that, I have one remark to Richard Musgrave. It was a habilitation thesis by Karl Homann, and he started from the premise where everything is collectively determined and then asked himself, how much do you privatize to get more and more efficiency so that the system works well? This may be the direction you are looking at?

Musgrave: I am looking at abundance, whether privately or publicly provided.

Bernholz: Yes, of course in the original setting there is no abundance at all. It is true. But I have some questions really for James Buchanan here. The first question concerns the limitation of your discussion to the problem of majority rule. Now that is an old problem already dealt with in the works by Montesquieu and other people. What I have really missed is the question that you have powerful minorities with rationally uninformed voters, you see. How does this fit into your scheme? That is the first question. The second question I have concerns your concept of the domain restrictions. I would have expected something different for this concept—namely, that the domain where the democratic principle is used to make decisions is limited—whereas in the way you have defined it in what you said is that it is the domain of rules that is applicable—namely, the ingenerality. By the way, this reminds me very much of the old rules of German public finance theory, where we had the *Allgemeinheit der Besteuerung* and other rules, you see. So I would say you are returning in a sense to these old rules. But isn't there also a proposal to limit the domain where you should apply majority voting as a principle, thus, in this sense to limit the domain of the government? Third, I always wonder how do you get to such a constitution. We have discussed that problem before, but we have not discussed it at all here. Finally, you haven't addressed the problem of the dynamics of the system: how it develops over time. Usually we begin with a rather limited domain of the government and then it starts extending, and then finally the system seems to enter some crisis. I was thinking of Sweden, for instance, or New Zealand, or also Britain before Thatcher. Then you get some reform and this reform has also to be explained in the public choice setting. What about your proposals? How do they fit into these developments?

William Niskanen, Cato Institute: It is important to recognize Buchanan's quite distinctive approach to taxes. Most conventional public finance focuses on minimizing the distortions in the private sector for a given amount of tax revenues. James Buchanan turns that completely around by saying: choose the taxes that minimize the distortions of public decisions. The problem is that different types of taxes are necessary to minimize the distortion of different types of government decisions. He has today proposed the combination of a demogrant and a proportional tax to minimize the distortions in the transfer state. But Lindhal, Buchanan, and Musgrave have recognized that a different type of tax is necessary to minimize the distortions in the productive state. A Lindhal tax is not necessarily proportional: it may be progressive, it may be less than proportional. One implication is that you might have to have different states: a distributive state that uses one type of tax system and a productive state that uses a different type of tax system. So, in effect, you take Musgrave's different functions of the states and you make them different states with different kinds of tax systems to minimize the distortions in the public decision making within these states.

One proposal that was made twenty-five years ago by Richard Zeckhauser combines the Buchanan perspective on redistribution and the concern about the tax on the private economy. Zeckhauser, from a veil of ignorance model, suggests that people would choose a tax system with the following characteristics: it would have a demogrant plus a tax system that has increasing average tax rates but declining marginal tax rates over the whole income distribution. Zeckhauser's tax-transfer formula is $-a + by - cy^2$. It is an interesting parabolic tax-transfer system where $-a$ is the demogrant and the tax system itself is then described as $by - cy^2$. It is a particular approach, slightly modifying Buchanan's approach of the demogrant plus a proportional tax.

A particular approach that tries to achieve the same outcome but minimizes the consequences on the private sector at the same time.

Most of us who have worked as public finance economists treat the government as exogenous and then try to minimize its effects on the private sector, whereas James Buchanan quite correctly treats the government as endogenous. In that case, it is important to choose taxes that minimize the distortions in the public sector. Two types of challenge remain. One is that we have different kinds of taxes that are necessary to minimize the distortions in different parts of the public sector, and second is that tax systems that minimize the distortions in one sector may not minimize the distortions in the other sector. In other words, tax systems that minimize the distortions in the public sector may not minimize the distortions in the private sector. We have to sort these out.

Sinn: Thank you for these interesting questions. James Buchanan, would you like to answer?

Buchanan: As for global or social utility or social welfare, I am not willing to impose any sort of a maximand. I am willing to acknowledge that the consequences of a rule, as you predict the pattern of outcomes, may in fact affect your evaluation of the rule. I am not happy with trying to force that through a single maximand because it seems to me that anybody who takes the view that I do, which is basically normative individualism, thinks that whatever emerges from individual choices emerges, and it is not a question of imposing a kind of global maximization process. I don't think that that is proper or possible. Now let me just go back and talk a little bit about several of Richard Musgrave's points. I have already talked about the benefit taxation point. I acknowledge fully his criticism to the effect that the meaning of discrimination, and nondiscrimination, is critically important. But let me emphasize, it is more important in an analytical exercise to try to define what the target is than it is to evaluate existing changes in programs. I submit that it is much easier for us if a political change is proposed. It is much easier to say that is in the direction of nondiscrimination, rather than the opposite direction. I think he and I would fully agree that the 1986 tax reform in the United States was in the direction of eliminating discrimination. The post-1986 changes from that '86 legislation have been in the direction toward more discrimination. Now it is much easier to set up criteria that allow us to determine the direction of change even though we may not be able to actually define what the target is in the ultimate sense. I won't really comment on his more general point about majoritarianism except to say that I don't think there is any sort of slippage in my own normative structure toward thinking majority rule is somehow good. I don't think it is good. I think maybe it is the least bad in some types of circumstances. We could get into a generalized discussion about majoritarianism versus nonmajoritarianism, but I think that would take too long and would get us over into political philosophy. I do acknowledge, and this is implicit in what I have already said, that I have moved in the direction of seeing more scope for general taxation than I did when I was more under the influence of the Wicksellian model. I did a piece, as you remember at a conference I believe that you, Richard Musgrave, organized that was called "Taxation and Fiscal Exchange." There I was explicitly spelling out the full implications of the Wicksellian model. I have moved in the direction, in your direction if you want to put it that way, and I now see a role for general taxation. Out of this comes the argument, if you can solve the benefit taxation problem that there is a case for using very general rules with the nondiscrimination part added to it. So I don't deny that I have moved in that direction. Now a more general point, and I will finish here. I thought your initial metaphor about me starting in the jungle and you starting in heaven is a good one, actually. Other people here have said, underneath it all I am influenced a great deal by Hobbes, and it may well be true. I fully accept that although Frans van Winden was saying here: I am also influenced by Spinoza; so those two ought to be put on equal terms perhaps in this respect.

Sinn: Yes, thank you. So, more questions. Peter Friedrich was the next.

Peter Friedrich, University of the Bundeswehr, Munich: I doubt whether the example of discrimination in figure 1 is a very good one, with respect to Alternative II, because why should we have a coalition between A and B against C, and not between B and C against A, and A and C against B. That means by reshuffling the benefits a little, one of the participants can convince a partner in the coalition to leave the coalition and to form a coalition with him. We have a kind of cycle. But if that is the case, then all three together would lose three net benefit points. If that is the alternative, they might form a coalition that is Alternative I by applying the "split the difference principle." Therefore, I think your Alternative II is not the best example of discrimination. We should reconstruct your example.

Buchanan: I fully acknowledge everything you say. Of course, I said the AB coalition is equally possible. You pick any one and you are absolutely right there will always be a continuous cycle in that particular model, and what you are proposing is that that they would agree and therefore to go back to Alternative I. That is precisely the von Neumann-

Morgenstern solution, but in the solution set there is always an advantage to a majority breaking out of that solution set. Now that solution set no doubt does have some elements of stability in it, but the game theorists don't accept it in the sense that you can't build it up as a viable stable solution. David Hume's defense of private property is related. I won't violate your property because I realize that if everybody did that, the whole world would fall apart. But, especially in the large number setting, you are much more likely to default. This is just a simple little stylized model. In a large number setting, it seems to me that clearly that solution set won't work. If you literally had a three-person set, you probably would get that as a solution.

Sinn: Is there someone else on this voting problem? No. Claude Hillinger is then coming with another question.

Claude Hillinger, University of Munich: James Buchanan is concerned with constitutional restrictions on the ability of a majority to exploit a minority. This concern can be traced back to the early stages of democratization, when the propertied minority was afraid of being expropriated by the propertyless majority. Two principal devices were employed to protect minorities generally, and the propertied class in particular: restrictions on the right to vote, particularly making it dependent on the ownership of property. This type of restriction no longer plays a role. The other device, still very much in evidence, is the division of power, not only among the institutions specified in the constitution but, in addition, among those whose development was not even foreseen—specifically, bureaucracies, pressure groups, and political parties. The current situation is characterized by the paradox that, while modern governments have rightly or wrongly assumed immense responsibility, they are unable to discharge these responsibilities in an intelligent, transparent, and democratic fashion. Today's majorities are frustrated and alienated from the political process, because they feel that they can exert no real influence. True, at election time they can "throw the rascals out," in favor of another cast of professional politicians—they may even elect a demagogic outsider; the effect on the future decision is marginal and unpredictable. The powerlessness of the electorate is mirrored by the distribution of power in modern, hierarchical political systems. Power is always rising to the top. For example, in the German system the voters feel relatively powerless. The communes feel powerless because they are regulated in great detail from above. The states, like Bavaria, feel relatively powerless. The Ministerpräsident of Bavaria wants the regions to have more power in the European system, but I think there is no way they can really get it. Within the nation state power is concentrated at the top, but we are getting the European Union and the common perception is that the individual nation-state does not have much power, because it is being regulated from Brussels. Buchanan made the point that our democracies are modified inheritances from the systems of hereditary rule of kings and aristocracies. I think we have not modified them enough. Specifically, the hereditary rule was characterized by the concentration of power at the top, because it was taken there by force of arms. Today, power is still at the top, and the possibilities for constitutional change are so difficult that the voters and the institutions at the lower level essentially feel powerless to change the system. I think that this is the basic source of the political dissatisfaction that we experience.

Sinn: Yes. Thank you, Fritz Schneider.

Fritz Schneider, University of Linz: Just a short question for James Buchanan. Are you really convinced that with the system you propose you can avoid rent seeking? I would doubt this. First, who sets up the flat tax rate, and on what—on income, capital income—what is the tax base here? This might be crucial. Second, who decides and who can change it again? Do you assume in your model that the government with the majority in the parliament or in two chambers decides on the level of taxes and the flat tax rate is sufficient to finance all state activities? I am somewhat puzzled why you don't consider the constraint of government directly by voting and the exit option. Let's see what happens when our system is not very vulnerable to rent seeking because of the exit option at least for part of the voters and taxpayers.

Sinn: Jim Buchanan, would you like to answer?

Buchanan: Yes, I can answer both those comments, in a way. I don't think that I would argue that in fact the proposal would eliminate rent seeking. You will get rent seeking. You have people trying to push around the level of the tax and the demogrant if you leave it within the ordinary democratic politics. And also, no doubt, it would arise in terms of definition of income. I deliberately left out the exit option aspect. As I said at the end, I am sure Richard Musgrave will have something to say about this in his talk tomorrow. We were talking about it in the press conference the other day. To the extent that the exit option operates, that will in fact modify how you might want to define what is the base for the flat tax. The exit option may, in fact, have an influence here in feeding back on this problem. As far as the problem about whether or not this would finance all public services: in a way, that is the same problem that I addressed before. The hardest thing to handle here is whether or not you want to earmark taxes for particularized targeted programs.

Let me go to the other comment here earlier. I do think you have to make a distinction between what is selfishness and self-interest in this context. The whole construction, a sort of constitutionalist construction, involves trying to develop the bridge between individual self-interest and "the general interest." By concentrating on the selection rules in which the individual is not really identified, we are engaged in the Rawlsian enterprise. It is the enterprise that we are involved in *The Calculus of Consent* and elsewhere, where in a sense a person is still operating within self-interest because that is the way we model individuals: that is not to say that an individual knows what his self interest is in the selfishness aspect. Victor Vanberg has talked about this. An individual always has a constitutional interest, that is an interest in the rules under which he is going to live. He has an active interest that may be the interest in a particular constitution. There you get a distinction between individual and constitutional interest. It relates back to what Peter Bernholz was raising about how do you get these constitutional reforms. Admittedly, there is not as much motivation for entrepreneurship at the level of constitutional reform and that creates a major problem in how do you get constitutional reform motivated.

Musgrave: Most people who favor a flat tax will allow for an exemption. Now if you allow an exemption in a flat tax, then you have a rising effective rate because the given exemption becomes smaller and smaller relative to income as you move up the income scale. Therefore, the flat tax with an exemption retains a progressive effective rate up to, say, the middle of the income scale, at which point it levels off and approaches the flat rate asymptotically. But in order to maintain effective rate progression higher up, rising bracket rates would still be needed. Otherwise, holding revenue constant, substituting the flat tax would result in shifting the burden massively from the upper third to the middle of the income scale. This downward shift in the burden would be pushed further if, as James Buchanan seems to suggest, the personal exemption was repealed.

Sinn: Gerold Krause-Junk, I believe you also want to speak on the flat rate. Is that true?

Gerold Krause-Junk, University of Hamburg: Yes, I am sorry, I would like to come back to two of the issues that have already been raised several times. First, a more general point. I think it is an old dream of mankind to set rules once and for all and then let the world go on peacefully and happily. I think the first reference might be the Ten Commandments and see what a bunch of people has been working since then on interpreting these rules. What I would like to say, or what I would like to think about is this: the more general rules are, the more people are involved in interpreting these rules, and the more specific they are, the sooner they get outdated and we have to try to find new rules. Therefore, I think this dream is an interesting one but it is not the answer to our problems. We probably have to have rules and policy within these rules. We have to try to get the best mix between autonomy and automatism. The other point I want to go back to is, of course, the flat rate tax. The flat rate tax has several names. I think it is also some part of the negative income tax and the demogrant or Bürgergeld in German, which is money handed out to every citizen. I have one objection against that kind of tax. It is about the opposite of what optimal taxation tells us taxes should be like. Optimal taxation clearly tells us the best tax is a lump-sum tax. With a demogrant, we are doing the opposite: we are distributing lump sum grants and then trying to get that back by marginal taxes on economic activities. Therefore, we maximize disincentives by such a rule, and it is also a very expensive tax. You have to hand out a terrible lot of money in the first place and you will be sure, at least that is what we think, that many people just would stop thinking about work; they would be very modest and take the demogrant and that is it. It is also a very dangerous thing for policy because the topic number one in the election might be to raise the demogrant, and therefore I have some hesitation in agreeing with this kind of theory, flat tax or simple tax.

Sinn: Peter Bernholz, yes, sure you can. I am looking at my watch. I think we have to come to an end as much as I would like to continue. You have a very urgent point? OK.

Bernholz: Well, the first question is addressed to James Buchanan. Wouldn't a progressive income tax really fit into your scheme if you had it in the constitution and if the schedule could not be changed by the parliament? The second question is addressed to Richard Musgrave. What do you do if you have a progressive income tax but if per capita income is increasing all the time and more and more people are driven into the higher progressive ranges?

Sinn: Yes, OK, may we have a final round with our two speakers and then we end.

Musgrave: Would you put the question again?

Bernholz: Well, modern economies grow all the time and per capita incomes are increasing all the time. With rising per capita incomes more and more people are driven into the upper scales of the progressive income tax. What do you do to correct that? Do you have a rule for that?

Musgrave: The answer is quite simple. The progressive rate schedule should relate effective rates to relative positions on the income scale. Obviously you are not going to set exemptions and bracket rates and let them stand for a hundred years. The rule, if you want to have one, is to change them in relation to average income. A new technique that is now used in the United States is to grant low-income support via an earned income credit that in effect, grants a subsidy to earnings at the low end of the scale and thereby leaves a favorable substitution effect.

Buchanan: An important aspect of the debate here is summarized in the comment that Richard Musgrave just made and [in those] several commentators have made implicitly, and that is what is the more attractive or least attractive. I think of this as a particular aspect of the tax structure. This distinguishes, I think, our position very clearly one from the other. I am not talking about what is or is not attractive. I am not trying to impose any normative preference, that is, whether I like a progression rate or a flat rate or whatever it might be or this or that. I mean I am willing to let that emerge from the majoritarian processes. Now majoritarian processes properly interpreted might well generate a huge public sector, but I am not concerned with that. What I am concerned with, and it may not be acceptable on those grounds, but what I am really concerned with, and this gets back to the jungle versus the heaven point: my concern and my primary motivation here in a normative sense is preventing the exploitation of man by man, or woman by woman, through the political process. That is what is driving my whole approach. It is not whether we want particularized progression or regression or what it might be in the direction of this or that.

Sinn: Yes, thank you very much. This was an excellent performance. Let's thank all speakers.

Day 4 (26 March 1998)

4.1

Fiscal Federalism

Richard A. Musgrave

I Introduction

The problems bundled together under the heading "fiscal federalism" deal with the spatial arrangement of fiscal affairs and their ordering in various jurisdictional settings. This is brought out most clearly if we imagine a unitary state that has to consider what fiscal functions are to be performed in centralized or decentralized fashion. Next, that analysis is adapted to a federalist setting where previously separate states form a union and consider how close that union and the conduct of fiscal functions are to be—that is, the position of the United States of 1788 and of Europe today. Finally, concern is with the relation between independent nation states, and the interaction of their fiscal systems. When moving from the first over the second and to the third setting, considerations of economic efficiency increasingly give way to those of retaining or surrendering national autonomy. Key issues that arise in the process include the now popular demand for decentralization (devolution in the United States, subsidiarity in the European Union) as a basic goal and the case for fiscal competition as against coordination as an ordering device.

II Fiscal Structure in the Unitary State

In line with what has been referred to as the "Musgravian" approach to fiscal federalism" (Rubinfeld 1987), the issues that arise and the policy conclusions that follow once more differ with the various functions that the fiscal system has to perform.

Provision for Public Goods

The general theory of public goods distinguishes between various characteristics that cause market failure and hence call for public provision. In the case of "pure public goods," such provision is called for because consumption is nonrival (in joint supply) and exclusion is inapplicable. In the case of "club goods," crowding introduces rivalry in consumption and excludability permits participants to be charged. Mixed goods arise where these features are combined in varying degrees. Placed in the context of fiscal federalism, a further factor of central importance enters. Pure public goods differ in benefit range, and participation in club goods requires a common location.

To secure an efficient outcome, the provision of public services should be determined and paid for by those who benefit. Public goods and services with nationwide benefit reach should be provided and paid for centrally, while those with local benefit reach should be provided for locally. Where preferences differ, the efficient arrangement would place people with similar preferences in the same regional or local service unit. The principle is clear but becomes complicated in application. Benefit intensities differ in reach for different services, and benefit spaces may overlap. Detailed mapping would thus call for a maze of service units, creating excessive costs of administration and surpassing administrative feasibility. Hence compromises are called for in designing a limited set of regional and local units. A minimum of three benefit ranges—nationwide, regional, and local—might be distinguished, and the provision of different services be assigned accordingly. Fiscal jurisdictions of varying sizes would be called for, but they would not, as in the federation, have to be ranked in hierarchical order from the center down.

The efficient spatial arrangement thus follows from the basket of public goods that are demanded and their spatial characteristics. From this, an important conclusion emerges that is relevant to the current debate over devolution (U.S.) and subsidiarity (E.U.). In the context of the model considered here—the efficient arrangement of fiscal jurisdictions in a unitary state—there is no presumption in favor of either centralized or decentralized provision of public goods. Provision should be decided by its consumers, since it is they "who know best" what is wanted. This, however, does not create a prima facie case for local or decentralized provision. The consumer group that knows best may be nationwide, regional or local, depending on what the spatial characteristics of the good happen to be and on how diverse preferences are.

A general presumption in favor of decentralization must thus rest on other grounds. Decentralized and hence smaller units of government may pay more attention to consumer preferences, or smaller government may be more competent or less corrupt, propositions that I question. On the contrary, fragmentation may be inefficient for administration and production economies. A larger number of governments, however, gives more options for exit and thereby may do better in restraining Leviathan where it exists (Brennan and Buchanan 1980, chap. 9), and it also leaves more scope for intergovernmental competition.

The matching of benefit reach with the spatial design of fiscal jurisdictions offers an efficiency rule, and it also suggests a marketlike mechanism of implementation. As Charles Tiebout first suggested in a paper in my Ann Arbor seminar in 1956, not only would the efficient solution call for people with the same preferences to share the same unit, but this would also be brought about by a "voting with the feet" process. People of similar preferences would find it advantageous to join in a particular location, so as to share in the costs of a uniformly desired public service, just as public-service providers would seek to attract such a group of consumers. Competition between and for fiscal units thus offers a useful ordering device, even where not needed to shackle an unruly Leviathan.

The proposition that voting with the feet generates an efficient outcome is intriguing, but a voluminous literature has pointed to serious limitations:

1. Taxation in Tiebout's formulation (Tiebout 1956) was in head tax form and hence nondistortionary, but local finance (where truly local) typically uses property taxation. If assessment is in relation to services rendered, property taxation remains a nondistortionary benefit tax. Where that linkage does not apply, it becomes a tax on capital. Capital, in the longer run, is mobile so that net returns are equalized across jurisdictions and resource allocation is distorted.

2. Tiebout's original formulation also assumed earnings to be independent of location choice. This assumption may hold in a suburban setting where income is earned centrally

while suburbs offer a choice of residency, but it no longer holds as the scenario shifts to a regional or national setting. There, location choice largely becomes a matter of job availability and is no longer fiscally conditioned.

3. The relation between income and residency is further broken once capital income is allowed for. Residents in high benefit and tax jurisdictions may choose to invest in low tax jurisdictions. Voting with the feet is now performed by capital seeking low tax rates rather than by residents seeking efficient budgets.

4. Tiebout's initial model also assumed that people have equal incomes. As income differences are allowed for, the nature of public goods renders it advantageous to reside with others not only of similar tastes but also of higher income. High-income neighbors will contribute more to the cost of public goods and thus reduce their cost to others. Location choice based on this gain may interfere with that called for by an efficient matching of labor and natural resources.

5. Moreover, low-income residents will follow the rich, while high-income residents will flee the poor, thus creating an unstable situation.

6. With regard to the provision of club-type public goods, there also arises the question of whether the efficient level of charges will suffice to meet the cost of optimal provision. If not, competition in the provision of public goods fails for the same reason as does private competition in the presence of decreasing costs (Sinn 1997).

Tiebout's model, calling for coresidence of people with the same tastes, correctly defines an efficient outcome, but voting with feet as an efficient ordering device has only limited applicability. The spatial allocation of service functions does not come about automatically but must be implemented by policy design.

The design calls for expenditures to be chosen and taxes to be paid where the benefits accrue. Tax burdens should not be exported to the outside. In the absence of strict benefit taxation, local finance, therefore, should draw on immobile factors, leaving taxation of mobile factors to central finance.

Distribution

Turning now to matters of distribution policy, suppose first that the desired state of distribution is viewed in national terms, to be applied across the entire population. Correction needed to implement that state must then be made centrally. All individuals are included and their entire income (wherever it originates) must be reached. Distribution policy must then be a central function. If preferences regarding nationwide distribution differ, people must seek a consensus. The agreed-upon state must be implemented centrally, which is what has to happen in a functioning democratic society.

A case for local conduct of distribution policy, at least in theory, applies where individuals are concerned with the state of distribution among their neighbors and within their local community only, rather than with its nationwide state. Distribution may then be viewed as a local public good and therefore to be implemented locally. Though justified in principle, the question arises whether such an arrangement is practicable. If both the rich and the poor were divided equally between egalitarians and nonegalitarians, the egalitarians (rich and poor) might then join as would the nonegalitarians, with redistribution occurring in the former but not in the latter set. But this is hardly a realistic construct, and it is more likely that egalitarian policies within one location only would attract low-income residents from other locations and thus be self-defeating as a neighborhood policy. It would be feasible only if accompanied by zoning or limited mobility.

The conclusion remains that distributional concerns, including social insurance and progressive taxation, must be met largely, if not entirely, at the central level. Such is the case the more so since capital is highly mobile, and since the effectiveness of progressive income taxation requires that capital be reached. There thus exists a linkage between the two issues: centralization permits progressive taxation and redistribution, whereas decentralization interferes with them. Though usually not featured in the centralization-decentralization debate, distributional considerations enter as a major force.

Stabilization

It remains to ask where the stabilization function should be located. In a single and closed nation, with a nationwide and unimpeded market, there is a prima facie case for a single currency, controlled by a single central bank. Similarly, there is a case for centralized conduct of stabilizing fiscal policy. Localized conduct of either policy generates leakages that weaken their local impact while causing disturbance outside. Central policy may be directed to impact differentially on particular locations when needed, but its overall scope has to be set with the national economy in mind. As noted below, that problem will take new form in the context of the European Union.

Conclusions

The conclusions to be reached for the unitary state are as follows: (1) efficient provision of public services calls for provision in line with their benefit regions, without a general presumption in favor of either centralization or decentralization; (2) concerns with the nationwide state of distribution calls for central implementation; and (3) macropolicy as well is an essentially central function.

III   Fiscal Structure in the Federation

Different considerations arise as we turn to a federal setting—that is, one where existing and independent states have decided to join in a federation. Fiscal arrangements are now constrained by and must be adapted to the predetermined geographic and political structure. Its cohesiveness may differ widely, ranging from more closely knit federations such as the United States over loosely structured unions such as to be developed in the European Union on to special purpose agreements such as NATO.

Whereas in the unitary setting concern was with the spatial arrangement of fiscal affairs among individuals, we now have a setting where member jurisdictions (that is, groups of individuals as citizens of their state) enter as distinct agents. This does not imply an organic theory of state where the member states "as such" have fiscal wants; but it does mean that *groups* of individuals enter as distinct players with demands based on their own polity. Individuals now appear in two distinct roles, one as citizens of their member states and the other as joint citizens of the federation.

The fiscal relation between the center (now the federation or union) and its member jurisdictions (states, provinces, Länder, or cantons) becomes of primary importance, with the middle-local level arrangements a second tier to be decided upon by the respective member jurisdictions or "states."

Expenditure Functions

Benefit ranges still enter into the distribution of expenditure functions but must now be adapted to accommodate existing states. National defense, the basic infrastructure of legal institutions and federationwide highways are federal or central functions, while regional highway nets are primarily state, and town roads are local concerns. Redistributional programs will again require central direction. But services overlap and interact so that what seems primarily local becomes of state concern and what seems primarily statewide also gains central (federal or national) interest.

Nor is the problem one of benefit scope only. Over a wide range of functions such as education and health services, assignment is not determined simply by spatial benefit considerations but depends on the extent to which member states are willing to surrender home rule to the center and yield authority to their lower levels. Moreover, there need not be a neat division of functions between jurisdictions. Those at the higher level may delegate implementation of programs to lower levels, while retaining varying degrees of control. Programs conducted at lower levels may be financed by grants from higher levels. Jurisdictions at various levels may undertake joint programs, and so forth. The structure of federalism that emerges thus reflects a balance between the desire of member states to retain independence and diversity and their intent to form a more closely knit union. The fiscal design must accommodate itself to rather than override these broader considerations given by historic, ethnic, and linguistic concerns. Nevertheless, as time passes, concerns with fiscal efficiency also become a determining factor.

Tax Assignments

The assignment of expenditure functions also determines how much revenue is to be raised by the various levels of government and, hence, conditions the design of tax structure.

Two considerations enter. To begin, there is again the principle that spending jurisdictions should also be responsible for their finance. This follows as a matter of efficiency in program choice and as a matter of equity, interpersonal as well as interjurisdictional. On similar grounds, there should be no exporting of tax burdens. In addition, ease of administration enters into the assignment of various taxes to levels of government.

The personal income tax is generally used as a central revenue source, and for good reasons. As a vehicle of personal and ability-to-pay taxation, it should combine a taxpayer's income from all sources in a single base independent of how and where it is derived. This is done more easily at the central than at the state or local level, especially with regard to capital income, much of which tends to be derived outside the recipient's residence. Moreover, state income taxation, unless imposed at similar rates, may be avoided by change of residence. The personal income tax in its progressive form is the major source of redistribution on the revenue side of the fiscal system and thus belongs at the central level. The same would hold if it were to be replaced by a personalized and progressive expenditure tax. Centralization, as noted before, is supportive of redistributional policy whereas decentralization tends to impede it.

The corporation or company tax also belongs primarily to the center. Companies operate across states, which render it difficult for any one state to claim its appropriate income share. A first problem arises in how state A should treat profits that foreign companies (branches of companies resident in B, or their subsidiaries) derive from operations in A. A second problem is how A should treat profits derived by its resident corporations operating in B. Where companies operate in multiple states, the imputing of profits to source involves great technical difficulties and is only approximated by use of formula apportionment. In addition, there is the problem of how A should deal with taxes that its residents have paid to B. Unless foreign taxes imposed at source are allowed for at residence, state taxation at differential rates will distort capital flows and interfere with efficient capital use.

Resolving these issues involves problems of equity across companies as well as across jurisdictions. They may be overcome in part by requiring that state taxes be imposed at uniform rates, but even then a need for harmonization remains. Modest company taxation at the state level is called for to provide the states with a tax share in the profits derived by nonresidents within their borders, but beyond this company taxation is best left to the central level. Partial distribution of its revenue to member states may offer a compromise solution.

These difficulties arise to a smaller degree only in the use of general commodity taxes. The retail sales tax, as generally used by the states in the United States, has the advantage of not requiring border adjustments while being nondistorting, even if applied at different rates. The latter also holds for a value-added tax of the destination type, although in this case border adjustments are needed. To avoid the necessity for such adjustments under the value-added tax, it has to be of the origin form, but in this case distortions arise with differential rates of tax, since in a federation there can be no countervailing exchange rate adjustments.

The common use of property taxation as a means of local finance reflects its use as an instrument of benefit taxation, especially where the nature of public services is such that benefits accrue directly to adjoining real estate. Local use of property taxation is also appropriate in that it applies to an immobile part of the tax base. At the same time, such uses of property taxation are to be distinguished from a more general inclusion of wealth as a supplementary index of ability to pay, a context in which such taxation also becomes appropriate on a broader and national scale.

While particular taxes are more suitable to one or another level of government, it does not follow that all bases should be given exclusive assignment. Where use overlaps, joint administration and similarity of base design is advantageous. Revenue from a centrally imposed value-added tax or income taxes may be returned to the jurisdictions of collection/source fully or in part. As is the case in Germany, all major taxes (personal income, company income, and value-added tax) serve in some degree as a joint base.

Return of revenue to source does not generate interjurisdictional transfers. Rather, it permits the use of superior central forms of taxation in lower-level finance. It is thus to be distinguished from grants-in-aid, financed out of federationwide revenue and made to support programs of particular states.

Grants-in-Aid

Grants-in-aid may be made for a variety of reasons. They may be used generally to draw on central taxes to finance state outlays. By combining tax centralization with outlay decentralization, the linkage between the centralization/decentralization issue with that of redistribution/non-redistribution may be broken.

More specifically, grants may be designed to support and/or to equalize particular state programs; or, more generally, they may be made to equalize fiscal capacities across jurisdictions. To reach their objective, grants may take various forms, general or selective, matching or block, once-and-for-all or continuing (R. A. Musgrave 1961). General block grants are in line with a decentralized perspective, whereas more narrowly categorical and matching grants point toward centralized control.

Central support of selected lower-level programs may be called for where such programs generate external benefits not accounted for by the jurisdiction of origin, such as programs to reduce pollution. But grants may also be called for to support programs whose immediate impact is local but offer services the availability of which, from the central perspective, is seen to deserve national support—for example, programs directed at education, health, or the arts. In particular, availability of floor levels of certain services such as classroom space may be held desirable as a matter of categorical equity in interindividual distribution.

Grants are made also to equalize fiscal capacities or to reduce interjurisdictional inequalities. Funds are transferred from high capacity and low need jurisdictions to others of high need and low capacity. This may take the form of equalizing need-adjusted revenue obtained at a specified common level of tax rate. Such equalization grants have widespread use in countries such as Germany, Switzerland, Australia, and Canada and in selective form also in the United States. They are held desirable as a matter of interjurisdictional equity, especially where average levels of income or natural resource endowments and hence fiscal capacities and needs differ sharply. Or they may simply be demanded by poor jurisdictions, be it as a condition for joining the federation or for not seceding.

An alternative approach views grants as an instrument to secure interindividual equity across states and to foster efficiency by neutralizing fiscal effects on the choice of residency. Initially proposed in 1950 (Buchanan 1950), this approach has recently been resumed in the Canadian discussion (Boadway and Flatters 1982). The principle of horizontal equity (calling for equal treatment of people in equal positions) is to be extended from the national to the member jurisdiction level. Equal treatment is defined in terms of equal "net fiscal residuals" allowing for both tax burdens and expenditure benefits. In the absence of adjustmenals, residuals for people living in high-income jurisdictions are higher, for previously noted reasons, than those of their equals in low-income jurisdictions. Transfers should be made, therefore, from high- and low-income people living in high income jurisdictions to high- and low-income people in low-income jurisdictions. This may be implemented directly by interindividual transfers; or, the high-income state, after assessing its citizens by their amounts due may transfer its total assessment to the low-income state, which in turn will use it to make the corresponding equalization payments to its residents.

Whichever procedure is followed does not matter, but the logic of the plan requires that such interindividual adjustment be made. It is therefore surprising that its proponents only focus on the aggregate amount to be transferred, while leaving the paying and receiving jurisdictions free to raise the funds and to disburse the proceeds as they wish. If such is the case, there remains little reason for determining aggregate transfers in line with a rationale that has been discarded.

Proponents of this approach also overstate their case by claiming that it offers the only acceptable rationale for grants. Fiscal capacity equalization is rejected as based on an organic view of the state and therefore unacceptable on "first principle." Only individuals can have needs, as they argue, and not jurisdictions. This misinterprets fiscal capacity equalization. Needs, to be sure, are experienced by individuals, but—and this is the essence of the federalism problem—they are experienced by individuals in groups, that is, as citizens of particular member jurisdictions. As such, they represent the interests of their group, while as members of the federation they may seek to balance these interests in a federally equitable fashion. Failure to recognize this and the dual role of individuals misses what federalism is about.

IV Fiscal Interaction among Independent Nation-States

It remains to consider the interaction of fiscal systems among independent nation-states, with competition, harmonization, and equalization the three alternative modes. Both the expenditure and tax sides of the budget are involved, but taxation, and company taxation in particular, poses the major problem.

Competition or Harmonization?

The role of competition may be viewed as a device to secure optimal fiscal performance or, more modestly, as a device to check fiscal inefficiency. If market competition by firms provides consumers with what they want at least cost, why shouldn't the same principle also hold to exact efficient performance from competing governments? Will not poorly performing governments lose out while superior ones be rewarded? Though appealing, the analogy is misleading.

Intergovernmental competition, as noted before, can serve fiscal efficiency in a suburban setting where surrounding bedroom communities vie for residents of similar preferences and taxation is in lump-sum or benefit-tax form. That model however is not transferable to fiscal competition among national governments (P. Musgrave 1991). Taxation is no longer benefit based, and benefits may be received in one jurisdiction while income is derived and taxes are paid in another. Tax bases as well as consumers of public services are mobile and need not move together. Tax bases, equipped to vote with their own feet seek to escape fiscal obligations rather than to obtain efficient services. Competition among governments to render high-quality services may give way to competition for offering low tax rates aimed to attract mobile factors.

If all tax bases were equally mobile, no one base could benefit from public services at the cost of others, but they are not. Immobile land must accept whatever burden is imposed upon it . Labor, still relatively immobile, comes next while capital (and particularly financial capital) is free to move. As a result, capital can be taxed on a benefit basis only. Any one country attempting to impose a net tax will suffer capital flight until the net return is raised to that available elsewhere. To do so would be unwise as the revenue gain from retaining a higher rate would be more than offset by an income loss to labor owing to a reduction in the country's capital stock (Oates and Schwab 1991). Given perfectly competitive markets and capital mobility, taxation of capital will be driven down to its benefit level. While a higher level is maintained in actual practice, this may be taken to reflect market imperfections as well as a tacit agreement among countries to neutralize the threat of capital outflow by retaining a common floor level of taxation.

This reasoning, to be sure, applies to the taxation of capital income by the country of source only. Turning to the taxation of capital income by the country of residence, tax avoidance now takes the form of change in residence rather than in the location of investment. But as in the preceding case, that option again tends to be more readily available to recipients of capital income than to earners of labor income.

Alternative techniques are available, however, which permit an orderly inclusion of capital income in the base. The ability of source countries to partake in the taxation of capital income originating within their borders may agree, as they in effect tend to do, to apply a common modest rate of withholding tax. Difficulties of residency taxation similarly could be overcome by adopting a common set of rates but, far from complying with the spirit of subsidiarity, this would be in the nature of centralization. The preferable alternative is to seek harmonization by measures that neutralize the distorting effects of differential taxation such as mutual crediting of the other's tax. This, however, may be difficult to achieve since it requires reaching all capital income under residence-based taxation, thus leaving rate equalization the second-best solution.

Prospects

It would be nice, by way of concluding this paper, to prescribe the optimal fiscal structure in its spatial setting. Unfortunately, this cannot be done. While there are principles of efficiency and equity to be considered, historical and political settings enter and exert a decisive influence. The degree of closeness into which jurisdictions are prepared to enter is only in part, and perhaps in small part, a matter of economics. Lacking a general formula I will close with a few remarks on what I think should be done about federalism in the United States and with some questions about future arrangements in the European Union.

U.S. fiscal federalism for its first century and a half was a rather decentralized system. Public expenditures prior to the Great Depression accounted for 10 percent of GNP. Of this, expenditures originating at the federal level accounted for 30 percent of the total, state expenditures accounted for 15 percent, and local expenditures for over 50 percent, much as they had at the beginning of the century. Since then the expenditure to GNP ratio has risen to over 30 percent, and shares by levels are currently around 70, 20, and 10 percent. The federal share more than doubled, while state and local shares both declined. Some of this gain is accounted for by the rising weight of defense but mostly reflects the growing importance of social programs, especially the rise of social insurance following World War II, as well as rising transfers to the states. Paralleling the rising expenditure share went that of federal taxes, leading the personal income tax into its now dominant position.

The rise of the federal share was thus associated with the expansion of income taxation and of transfer payments, thereby linking central finance to big government and redistribution. Following half a century of fiscal activism and central leadership, the call now is for downsizing the federal budget and a devolution of fiscal responsibilities to the state and local levels. The federal weight is to be reduced, and grants are to be given in block, noncategorical, and nonmatching form, and without assurance as to whether and when such support will continue.

These trends reflect a response to excessively detailed federal directives, but that is not all. Behind the call for devolution of federal programs, if less audible, is also support for shifting from a superior and progressive federal tax system to relying on less equitable state and local taxation and to widening the scope for fiscal competition. Similarly, devolution not only aims at revising the weights carried by the higher levels of government but also carries an expectation that lower-level government means less government. Left with some degree of unease about these undercurrents, I would like to see U.S. federalism evolve in these directions:

1. Retention of the federal income tax as the mainstay of the tax system, along with a broadening of the base and simplification, especially over the lower- and middle-income range.

2. Integration of the federal corporation profits tax with the personal income tax.

3. Placing the definition of taxable income for state income taxes on the federal base, with joint collection and partial return of revenue to the states.

4. Application of state corporation taxes at a low uniform rate, combined with adoption of a uniform apportionment formula.

5. Extensive use of categorical grants, leaving substantial discretion over detailed program design to the states.

6. Conduct of grant programs on a continuing and stable, not ad hoc basis, with cyclical flexibility absorbed at the federal level.

Turning now to the European scene, we observe that the Euro is about to take over, and the first major chapter of unification is completed. What should happen next is not for me to recommend. Much will depend on to what degree the member states will wish to retain their separate identities or join into a closer union. There will hardly be a single state, with the role of France, England, and Germany reduced to provincial status, but there are many degrees and directions that further unification may take, and perhaps must take, to arrive at a viable system. The proposed structure is unique in that it combines a common market and currency in a setting of still limited labor mobility, and without providing for a significant central budget. I wonder whether this will prove to be a workable arrangement.

Surely there will be pressures from both tax and expenditure policy to move toward a more substantial central budget. As the share in economic activity that extends across the borders of the member states increases, involving both capital and labor, the use of residency-based taxation, conducted at different rates and patterns, becomes increasingly difficult. The choice then is between abandoning such taxes, at the cost of destroying the equity of the tax system, or requiring uniformity. If the latter, administrative ease calls for central administration, with return of revenue to source. Similar pressures toward centralization arise on the expenditure side of the budget, especially with regard to social services. Labor mobility is again a crucial factor. If benefits are linked to basic residency or nationality, claims would have to be portable to changing places of employment and be serviced across jurisdictions. If, instead, benefits are linked to location of employment, differential benefit levels will distort employment choice. The solution to the dilemma again points to a more uniform and centralized system. Globalization, decentralization, and diversity may prove to be uneasy partners. Finally, pressure toward a more active central budget may be expected to emerge as the poorer members of the federation call for some degree of fiscal equalization. Recognized already on a small scale, this is likely to gain weight as it has in other federation, and call for an increased share of revenue to accrue to the central budget.

The most puzzling problem, perhaps, is the future of stabilization policy. There is to be an E.U.-wide Central Bank but as now visualized, this allows no place for fiscal policy as an instrument of stabilization. There is no central budget large enough to make a difference, and such budget as prevails has to be balanced. The member states similarly are restrained by common deficit and debt limitations. The entire responsibility for stabilization is thus left with the common central bank and its monetary policy.

This raises the question whether monetary policy alone will always be adequate to deal with stabilization? Especially important in the E.U. context, there is also the question whether it will be suited adequately to deal with localized differences in economic conditions. So long as labor mobility is limited, such differences will prevail and may call for differential treatment. Conceivably, this might be met by regional differentiation in credit conditions but fiscal measures may also be required, and for this more freedom for budget policy would be needed by member states.

It thus remains to be seen whether the combination of unitary and decentralized features, now posited in the E.U. structure, will prove tenable—a fascinating experiment in federalism of importance not only to Europe but also elsewhere.

4.2 Response

James M. Buchanan

I had not known Richard Musgrave very long when I was delegated by the National Bureau of Economic Research in the United States to organize a conference on public spending. It was held in Charlottesville, Virginia, in 1959. At that conference, there were two papers on fiscal federalism, one by Musgrave and one by his student, Charles Tiebout. I was delegated to be the discussant of those papers. So after thirty-nine years we are back to where we were, and I suspect that there have not been all that many changes in our positions since then. It does seem to me that the fundamental distinction between Richard Musgrave's approach and my own can be described as follows. I approach the whole problem of federalism from the point of view of political philosophy, whereas he approaches it very much from the point of view of a fiscal economist. I think that comes out very clearly in our reaction to the raised sets of issues. I have always looked on federalism as a means by which you can restrict or have some control, through built-in institutions that will control the power of the government.

The very fact that Musgrave started out the discussion by the three perspectives—namely, the unitary state, the federation, and the set of autonomous nation-states, as the three possible starting points—suggests that he presupposes the political structure; whereas my whole approach involves trying to set up a kind of normative evaluation of alternative types of political structure. I am not willing to presuppose a political structure. It seems to me the whole federalism question comes up when you are trying to imagine setting up the ultimate political institutions. From the perspective that I take, what is and what is not necessarily the most efficient arrangement is really only one element in the picture. There are trade-offs between efficiency and what you might call control of the political authority, efficiency in a larger sense, but it is not efficiency in the narrow fiscal economist sense. Even if division of powers between the central government and a set of local governments should not be efficient, there would still be an argument in favor of delegating some power to those governments as a means of controlling or checking the central government authority. So within some threshold, you would still want a federal structure.

I am not going to spend really much time in my response here talking about the problem of equalizing federal grants between regions or parts of a government. I did develop one approach a long time ago in which I tried to derive some logic of an organizational model of different jurisdictions. I could defend that in another way, but whether or not you want to have a set of equalizing grants in the units in a federation will depend on whether or not you want to put the full burden of adjustment on mobility of your factors or whether you somehow want to offset that. It seems to me that there is an argument, and there might be an argument in Europe that will be forthcoming that you may want to have a set of equalizing grants in order to accomplish roughly some sort of equalization in fiscal capacities as among regions. Of course, many of my libertarian friends would object very strongly to that, but I think there is an argument against it and an argument for it. One argument against it can be illustrated with the example with Canada. Canada has had a set of these kind of equalizing grants for quite a long time, but the main beneficiaries of those grants have been the maritime provinces. The maritime provinces in Canada have come to be in a dependency status with vis-a-vis the rest of Canada. In a sense, over time that is a major objection to any sort of equalizing grant. Whether or not you want to put the full burden of adjustment on the mobility of your factors in this fiscal arrangement or federal arrangements is, I think, the critical question.

The real issue between us, in particular, is on the whole notion of competitive governments or fiscal competition. Again, I don't look on this necessarily as an efficiency problem in the strict analogue to a market economy. I look on it to the extent that you have effective competition among governments. In a sense, you are giving people, individuals, as resource owners and as residents, an exit option. If there is an exit option, if there is a chance to leave, this necessarily imposes discipline on those who would exploit you through a political structure or a bureaucratic structure. I think one thing that Musgrave fears is that if you have effective inter-jurisdictional competition, it is going to be impossible for any one particular jurisdiction to be grossly inefficient, relative to the other units in the integrated network or the integrated nexus. There is no way you can deny that, and in one sense I think those who are opposed to fiscal competition really are saying indirectly that we want a jurisdiction to be inefficient in the strict sense of economic efficiency. That is where the debate is really joined, it seems to me, and of course I favor that because it does necessarily impose limits.

I think it is often overlooked in the European context, in
particular, that people fear, understandably so, the centralization of authority in Brussels, and they are very concerned
about that—namely, those who oppose movements toward
European federation. What they don't recognize is that as
in fact you move toward federalism or federation you are
restricting and perhaps restricting severely the power of
your own local politicians and bureaucrats to impose cost
on you. So it is a trade-off again as you move toward a
federal structure.

I want to talk a little about my own experience with the
European possibilities and prospects. In 1990, I was invited
to prepare a paper for a conference in Paris. I think it was
February 1990 when I went and gave that paper, which I
called "Europe's Constitutional Opportunity." I was very
surprised. I was making essentially the argument for a competitive federalism, that is, a very optimistic aspect of looking at Europe as a competitive federal structure. What I was
surprised at was that I was violently attacked from both
sides of the spectrum, which made me think I must have
been right. If anything, I was attacked even more violently
by the right, if you would call it that, than by the left, but I
was attacked also by the left. I was attacked by the right
mostly by Britishers who at that time had formed what they
called the Bruges Group. There were a few European members in that group, but basically it was dominated by the
British. They really did make some ad hominum type at-
tacks on me. I was a vicious man because I was proposing
the possibility that Europe was moving toward some sort of
federal structure. "Federal" is a black word in their lexicon;
the idea of federalism or federation or anything like that
they consider outrageous. They were essentially refusing to
agree to have England or Britain give up even one jot of

what they thought was their national sovereignty. They completely failed to understand the advantages or logic of a federal structure. I was equally attacked though not quite in such personal terms by those on the left, essentially the Delors Brussels position, which again surprised me because I thought that by 1990 clearly the lesson had been learned that socialism was not working. But they were attacking me because they opposed competition. They very strongly opposed the competition in a federalism that I was suggesting because they were eager to direct and manage everything from Brussels. The *dirigisme* mentality was very strong. So I was in between. I gave this paper several times in different versions and the same thing happened over again. Then along came Maastricht, which, of course, was dominated by the *dirigistes* from Brussels. That is implicit in the whole Maastricht treaty. Its supporters had forgotten about the great advantages that Europe might have from genuine competitive federalism. They don't like competitive federalism on basically the same ground I think Musgrave doesn't like it. And it seems that Europe in one sense did miss out in part on its constitutional opportunity. But maybe the forces of history are going to work out that way after all.

I think Europe did miss out on a wonderful opportunity to introduce a really good monetary structure. It seems to me that Europe in the early nineties had the chance of adopting a proposal for competitive currencies. All that would have been needed would have been something in the treaties that would have allowed any citizen of any country in Europe to make contracts, including paying taxes, in any money that is issued by any bank in the structure. In that context, the separate central banks could still operate, and you could still have the local currencies, but in fact they would be in competition, so no central bank would dare inflate the currency because it would essentially lose out, and therefore you would have discipline imposed by competition on the separate banks. At the same time, people could have still retained their traditional currencies. Instead, Maastricht tore up that kind of possibility and they moved toward the Euro. I think Europe missed out on a wonderful opportunity. But having made that commitment and moving along to where you are now (Buchanan 1998), I think if I were a European I would be in favor of going ahead, despite all the problems. It seems to me it's like Macbeth. "I am in blood steeped in so far, that should I wade no more, returning were as dangerous as go o'er" or something like that. So it seems to me that if I were European now, I would be in favor of going ahead with the Euro despite the fact that you missed out on the other opportunity. And I can understand Chancellor Kohl's position on this. He is not being dominated at all by the economic issues; he is quoted as saying "nationalism is war."

Many people do feel that Europe must, in fact, move toward some sort of integrated structure. The danger, of course, is that the Brussels bureaucracy will dominate and that you will have excessive harmonization and regularization, which would mean a less prosperous Europe. However, it seems to me that the bureaucracy in Brussels cannot in fact determine where history is going to head. If I were predicting about Europe, I think the differences in the languages and traditions are such that a competitive federalism of sorts is almost going to necessarily emerge. The forces of history are almost going to guarantee it. I like to think of a federal structure in the following way, and I think it is applicable in the European context: Think of a satellite in orbit. A satellite in orbit is, of course, being maintained by the centripetal and centrifugal forces in equilibrium. So you can sort of think of federalism as a satellite being pulled always by two separate forces in opposite directions— namely, a force toward monolithic centralized authority and forces in the other direction toward a set of autonomous separate units. So federalism is a kind of equilibrium. It is shaky to maintain that equilibrium, but I think in the European context it may be the future likelihood or prospect.

Now let me end up by just saying a few words about the death of the nation-state. I think you can make an argument that maybe there are some functions of the traditional nation-state boundaries that are becoming obsolete at that level. I think the question here is basically an empirical question. Is the national community the size community that is going to command the required loyalties of individuals? Without an external enemy, can you maintain the sense of community in the particularized political unit that happens to be existent? Israel provides a clear exception. They obviously still have a very strong external enemy. As a consequence, the sense of community at the level of the nation-state is very strong. But certainly in my own country, it is very difficult to see how the American context of the United States has much sense of community about itself. Germany, for example, may be quite different because you do have linguistics, but on the other hand you don't have much history. Germany has only been a nation-state for 150 years or so. At the end of the day, it is largely an empirical question as to whether or not these political nation-states are going to command the loyalties of people. Or are you going to have regions like Catalonia, for example, that are going to become more and more dominant. That is I think what is likely to be played out within the next few decades.

4.3 Discussion

Sinn: We have been talking about satellites and about the moon, but the real subject is the earth and here Europe. Europe is a very fascinating and important topic these days so, please, who wants to start?

Peter Bernholz, University of Basel: Let me first make a remark to James Buchanan. I have myself proposed this idea of currency competition based on individual rights, but I should add that at the same time we have empirical evidence that it works only if we have rather big differences of inflation. So I am very much in favor of such a right but we shouldn't overestimate what it can do.

I would also ask us to be modest as to our claims for fiscal federalism or what we know about it. As far as I know, we are not able to prove even on a very abstract level that spatial equilibria exist, you see. If you include now all the fiscal and tax expenditure problems we have, I guess we have to admit that we know very little about many aspects, and this is also true about this kind of competition.

I favor this kind of federal competition myself, and I think I have some arguments for it, but I have to admit, theoretically we have very many open questions. Let me therefore perhaps again state the main question with which we are faced. Of course it is quite clear, as both speakers have stressed, that this is not only an economic question. We have the question of cultural and other differences, which are very important here and which is why I speak in favor of federalism. Coming from Switzerland, [I find that] it would be impossible to imagine the centralized state there and the same would be true for a future Europe. I am here of exactly the same opinion as James Buchanan. I would even assert that Europe will be a success if it is in this sense decentralized, federalized, but that this will not happen if it is absolutely centralized.

That would be a prediction in line with James Buchanan's. I share his position on that point. Power corrupts, and this leads me to the theoretical basis. There are good arguments, and in Switzerland we would certainly start from that argument. We have to decentralize as a kind of separation of powers, you see, to contain the misuse of power by the people governing. Now, let me ask you the question that is more related to the economic aspect of it. I would say the question is really: How can an efficient tax expenditure system be developed which corresponds to the preferences of citizens given incomplete information? I think that is the problem, and we have two opposing proposals there. One is that of a central system which then has to be rationally constructed, because if you don't have competition, we cannot have search-the-system processes. We have to construct centrally, and this gives rise to very many problems. The pretension of knowledge, as Hayek would call it, would be implied by this constructivism, and with our present state of knowledge that is perhaps too much. On the other hand, we could have competition among jurisdictions. We might examine whether the competition among jurisdictions is not a discovery process with a certain possibility of detecting better systems, taking into account the preferences and wishes of the people. Of course, this only works with the help of the exit option. On the other hand, I don't deny that this leads to redistributional problems stressed by Musgrave. So we are faced with a host of problems, and I suppose we still don't have the answer to many of them.

Josef Falkinger, University of Regensburg: Professor Musgrave expressed his skeptical view about interfiscal competition, and Professor Buchanan stressed, on the other hand, the political merits of the opting out possibilities offered by competing jurisdictions. I think we don't have any choice other than to expand the spectrum of multiple jurisdiction. I want to come back to the taxation example you mentioned. You said an optimal tax system in a federal system should tax the immobile factors. But which immobile factors do we have? Capital is mobile. The more able workers are mobile. So you can tax land, you can tax less flexible workers. I mean, you will need an international tax system, sooner or later, in a world with mobile factors. Or if you want to prevent workers or people from moving by an international transfer system, then you need an international government implementing this transfer system. And you have global public rules and international rights, which have to be guaranteed if you want international economic activity. So I think there is no choice and we will need some international jurisdiction, and, actually, in some areas we have it already. So isn't the main task to design the constitution for this international jurisdiction? Political power can be limited by exit options but also by constitutions and by vote. Isn't the task we have to face for the future to design a constitution for the international jurisdiction rather than to say we don't want to have such a jurisdiction?

Buchanan: I agree fundamentally with your argument. I have been involved with the European Constitutional

Group and then with Frank Vibert, who has written a book on this proposing a constitution specifically for Europe. The way Europe is developing in its federalism structures is by a set of separate treaties and organizations, without any real thinking in terms of an integrated constitutional structure. I do agree with you fundamentally that that is desperately needed now in the European context. You need to sit down and have some sort of version of a constitutional convention, somehow, and lay it all out as a rational basis and that is really desperately needed, I think.

Musgrave: If you want to combine a minimal central government with fiscal competition, you may find that competition will lead to fiscal uniformity, similar in that respect to a centralized setting. To avoid this paradox, what is needed is a cooperative approach to tax policy that permits diversity but avoids the distorting effects of competition.

Sinn: I have now Frans van Winden, Dieter Biehl, William Niskanen, and Peter Bernholz again. I wish us to continue this line of discussion, so the question is: Is competition workable, what kind of centralized activities do we need, do we need a constitution to set the rules of the game, or do we even need more centralized government in the sense of Richard Musgrave? So assuming that it is on this topic, Frans van Winden, you may go to the microphone. If it is something else, please wait. Dieter Biehl, that issue?

Dieter Biehl, University of Frankfurt: My first claim is that there is something like an optimal intensity of competition. If you think in terms of a scale ranging from zero competition up to 100 percent competition—that is, a totally unrestricted competition—then both polar cases are cost-maximizing and, therefore, undesirable solutions, and the optimal solution lies somewhere in between these extremes.

We all know that even for private-sector competition, the 100 percent competition intensity does not exist and that all modern societies have restricted private competition to at least some degree. If I start from here and then go to the issue of intergovernmental including fiscal competition, I think that the same conclusion applies: Neither zero nor 100 percent competition is optimal. I think that this is in line with Richard Musgrave's argument that the European Community will have to create a constitutional framework that restricts but [does] not totally exclude fiscal competition within the EU—that, for example, Luxembourg can be "taxed" if it does not comply with certain rules concerning the tax treatment of banks and of interest income, or that the Netherlands can be hindered to attract headquarters of multinationals by lowering taxation only for this special category of enterprises. Such selective measures tend to cause distortions of locational competition among countries that participate in a common market. States that offer selective lower taxation naturally do not intend to give away tax claims but hope to attract new enterprises with a high tax capacity and/or a high employment capacity so that they will be better off in the long run. Less selective strategies do not always produce net benefits. A national strategy of general fiscal competition, in the sense that a country substantially reduces the level of all categories of expenditure and all types of taxes, is very difficult as it would imply a strong deviation from its traditional understanding of the role of the public sector. In addition, as long as the allocative fiscal residuum would not be changed significantly the success of such a strategy would be small. Such a strategy could work, however, if the intensity of the national welfare state transfer system is reduced. I therefore conclude that trying to realize an optimal intensity of intergovernmental competition through constitutional framing is one of the important issues that demonstrates the need for a constitutional solution at the EU level.

As far as the development of such a European constitution is concerned, I think that this cannot be done in a sort of "one-shot" exercise. Already in 1953, the enlarged Parliamentary Assembly of the European Community for Coal and Steel and, in 1983, the European Parliament elaborated draft proposals for a European Constitution. These attempts, however, have not been successful as the majority preferences among the countries concerned have been too heterogeneous. What has been successful was the strategy I call the interplay of the integration process and institutionalization. The first six member states started in 1951 with a sectoral community, the Community for Coal and Steel, for which a sufficiently strong consensus was obtained, but were unable to realize a political community and a defense community in the early fifties. Instead, in 1958 the European Economic Community was established. It then followed three enlargements, the European Single Act of 1986, the Maastricht Treaty of 1992 with the decision on the European Monetary Union, and the Amsterdam Treaty of 1997. I think that this interplay between the consensus-building integration process and institutionalization will continue to determine the development of the EU. As far as fiscal competition is concerned, the Treaty of Amsterdam contains some rules (cf. articles 87–93), but they do not deal explicitly with possible distortions of locational tax competition we are discussing here. This implies that these ideas will have to be discussed until a sufficient consensus is obtained.

Let me add a final remark on the nation-state issue in the context of the EU enlargement toward central and eastern Europe. The accession negotiations with up to ten countries will start soon. In all of these countries, national movements have contributed to ending the Soviet empire. However, this also implies that the nation-state issue is an important one and, in some of these countries, the relationship between national majorities and ethnic minorities are characterized rather by tensions than by consensus. This points to an increasing degree of heterogeneity for the near future and could possibly also reduce the chances for obtaining "constitutional" solutions in the field of fiscal competition.

Sinn: Yes, thank you. Peter Bernholz, also on this issue: fiscal competition versus centralization.

Bernholz: Well, with all due respect, Richard Musgrave, I would like to contradict your hypothesis that all the tax rates will be the same within a competitive system. We have now had cantonal income taxes in Switzerland for decades and the cantonal income tax is still much more important than the federal income tax and still we have very big differences. The canton of Zug has an income tax rate that is only half that of the highest canton tax. I think what is neglected in your hypothesis is first transaction costs for individuals that may be rather high with different languages, with different property prices and so on. Property prices are of course dependent on taxes again, and you also have different preferences and restrictions for individuals. So I don't see this development.

As to the European question, I would only like to say: of course, we need some centrally provided services and, in this sense, we need a central government. But the European Constitutional Group to which I belong has proposed to restrict it as much as possible to allow the discovery process of competition. Moreover, I would predict that, with the accession of several eastern European countries with rather low per capita incomes, the present transfer system will break down absolutely. The West Germans are already dissatisfied with the transfers to East Germany. Now look at the magnitude of the problem that is coming up, so the whole system will be changed. There will only be very limited transfers. Already we see the quarrel developing. Already you see the southern European parties, Spain and so on, fighting for the redistribution of the funds that are now available for transfers. So my prediction would be that we will have a very limited transfer system in this European Union, which is evolving.

Musgrave: The proposition that you will have these beneficial effects of competition means that exit costs are not that high, because if they were, then competition would not work.

Hartmut Fest, Ministry for Economics, Bonn: I must remind you, I am not an academic scholar though I have worked at the OECD in the Economics Directorate as a professional economist. My question is to both Professor Musgrave and Professor Buchanan. Have you followed the development of the sequence of draft proposals by the Commission on the harmonization of capital taxation? Whenever the Commission put forward a revised proposal, all finance ministers who clamored domestically that the tax base has been eroding came together and said: "Oh no, this is too touchy; we do not want to give up tax autonomy." Obviously, you can't have it both ways, and in order to arrive at some measure of coordination in capital tax policy across EU countries, all governments have to cede some of their capacity to tax or not to tax (e.g., capital gains). So in December last year, they convened again and finally signed a nonbinding resolution that sets out certain limits on possible tax rates and attempts to circumscribe what is called "unfair competition." But when you scrutinize the text, unfair competition is such a fuzzy notion that, in fact, you are even in a situation that appears to be worse than if some sort of watered-down draft proposal of the Commission of earlier vintage had been adopted. That is my first point. The second point is the following. Having been an active participant in, and an avid supporter of, the integration process in Brussels for some thirty years, I can tell you that Professor Buchanan's picture is the more likely outcome. There is a whole lot of socially nonproductive resources working at Brussels—that is, company lawyers, agencies monitoring sectoral trends, and big enterprise lobbying—looking at what the Commission is doing, well ahead of even governments. Mind you, Siemens or other big companies have quite a lot of professionals in various areas monitoring the Commission. Hence I would agree, there is a measure of irrationality or lack of rationality. I would be interested in your reaction to these problematic developments.

Musgrave: What you say is perfectly sound, but there has to be some division of labor and, as I mentioned in my first paper, the three-branch structure is useful when thinking about how to do things right. That doesn't mean that this is how they *will* be done. The practical man has the advantage of understanding how things are really done, and we may take the liberty of overlooking that, but unless we were to show him how things *should* be done, how would he know where to aim?

Reiner Eichenberger, University of Zurich: I doubt that the alleged negative aspects of tax competition can be overcome effectively by harmonizing taxes, because the governments have a lot of substitutes for competing with low taxes. When they cannot compete with taxes they will compete with subsidies; they will compete by selling land to firms below the market price and by overinvesting in clientele specific infrastructure and public services. This kind of competition shows all the alleged negative aspects of tax competition. Worst of all, it is costly, and the favors are mainly given to specific firms and well-organized interest groups. But there are no benefits to the general population in the form of lower taxes. Thus, I think that the realistic alternative to tax competition is much worse than tax competition itself.

Peggy Musgrave, University of California, Santa Cruz: With regard to fiscal competition, I think that it may be all to the good if the single fiscal function of federation members is to provide public services financed through pure benefit taxation. But if member states also have a redistributive function, either on the expenditure side or on the tax side, then fiscal competition will prevent them from applying that function. Put another way, if fiscal competition is accepted, then one must think in terms of the central (federal) authority being entirely responsible for redistributive taxation and expenditures.

William Niskanen, Cato Institute: Two details about the relationships between the national and regional governments can lead to an overexpansion of government. One is whether the transfers from the national government are in the form of grants to the local jurisdictions or transfers to the individuals involved. One might think the outcome would be identical if the state local governments treated money from the federal government in the same way as they treat additional spending power by their own parties. But the evidence is quite contrary to that. Richard Musgrave's own former colleagues at the University of Michigan have made the best estimates of this; they estimate that the marginal propensity for state local governments to spend out of personal income in the state is about 10 percent. But the marginal propensity for state local governments to spend out of grants from the federal government is in the order of 80–90 percent. They have named that the fly paper effect—money sticks where it lands. Now one might think that if the state local governments were strictly responding to the local political demands, $100 per capita of federal grants would lead to say $90 per capita tax reduction and $10 additional state spending, but it looks as if it is almost entirely the other way around in that it leads to $80 or $90 of additional state spending and $10–20 of reduced state local taxes. We need to pay more attention to the differential effects of grants and transfers. The implicit case for grants is that the national government is taking a paternalistic perspective about the people in the local jurisdictions, saying that they don't know what is good for them and they need more of certain kinds of spending than they would otherwise spend if we sent them the money. Now that is a very different perspective as compared to the fiscal equalization argument. The fiscal equalization argument would suggest that you send the money to the individuals and then they make their own collective decisions, within their own regions, about how much of that should be spent for particular goods and services provided by the local government. So first sending money in the form of grants to the states rather than transfers to the individuals can lead to a bigger government than would be the case if the money were sent to the individuals.

Second, a very important recent contribution has been made by Jean-Luc Migué of Quebec on competition between the national government and the local government. Most of our attention has been focused on competition among the regional governments, but Jean-Luc Migué has explored the implications of the national government competing with the regional government for the local voter pool. He concludes that there is a common pool problem, overexploitation of the local voter base, and this leads to too large government because they are both competing, in effect, for the same voter base and the same tax base, whereas competition among regional governments is competition across voter bases and across tax bases. If the federal constitution does not have a clear division of powers between the national government and the local governments, the federal government should be expected to compete with the local governments for the provision of what might otherwise be local government services—child care, schooling, crime control, whatever. That is the single best explanation for why in recent decades you don't find very much effect of federalism on total per capita government spending. One used to find a big difference between federal structures and unitary structures of government spending per capita; that is no longer the case. The primary reason for that, Migué suggests, is the erosion of the division of powers between the national government and the local governments. When you have that, you can have an overexpansion of the government. In the United States, we have seen that even in issues like crime. In the past ten or twenty years, we have had a federalization of the criminal code, the consequence of which is that the federal prosecutors and local prosecutors are now competing on how tough a sentence they can put on people. The implications of that for our civil liberties is that we have lost any meaningful protection against double jeopardy. We could be acquitted by a state court on a particular charge and then convicted in a federal court on the same body of evidence. That is a very dangerous development, but it is just a sideline of the general erosion of limits on the powers of the national governments in terms of the functions and the roles that they can perform.

Sinn: William, can you draw the conclusion from that for Europe?

Niskanen: The vision for Europe should be following: If there is to be a federal structure for Europe, you should try to do what Madison and his colleagues initially tried to do in the United States—to have a clear division of roles between the powers of the federal government and the powers of the regional governments. Once that division erodes, and the national government or the Europeanwide government and regional governments compete, then you can have an overexpenditure. The other implication is that unless you have a very paternalistic view about how much government spending ought to be for child care, for local public health, etc, from the Europeanwide point of view, fiscal equalization should be in the form of transfers to individuals and not grants to the local government.

Musgrave: I take a different view of fiscal equalization and the role of the flypaper effect. When the federal government makes grants to state governments, you would expect them to reduce their taxes, thereby transferring the grant to individuals who then can do with it what they want. But they don't. The grant sticks with the government that receives it, and this is considered unfortunate. Well, I am pleased that the flypaper effect exists. I am pleased because it allows the granting government to equalize fiscal capacities across lower-level jurisdictions. If its goal were to enhance the spending power of individuals, then it would make grants to them directly in line with their own means, and not with the average income of their jurisdictions. If the federal government makes grants to lower-level jurisdictions, it does this precisely to make use of the flypaper effect. It does not want to give the grants to individuals one by one, but to groups of individuals, as reflected by their membership in that particular jurisdiction; and it wants to give them to groups of individuals because it wants these grants to be directed at equalizing their capacity to render what it considers essential public goods. This gets us into the question of categorical equity. It makes sense for the federal government to make earmarked grants to lower-level jurisdictions if it thinks that the particular service function to which the grants are earmarked are justified in line with considerations of categorical equity. If grants are made as block grants, nonearmarked grants, that would be to equalize the capacity of lower-level governments to provide public goods in general, a less likely goal. In either case, the grants are not meant to be passed on to individuals who as members of the federation then make their choice. I think that misunderstands the nature of federalism and its concern with groups of individuals as citizens of their subjurisdictions.

Niskanen: Your position substitutes a national decision for how much local government should spend for a local government decision on how much local government should spend.

Musgrave: You affect how much various local governments can spend, and that is the equity purpose that the federal government undertakes in its grants policy. Much depends on how much cohesiveness you think there should be with the federation, to what extent the citizens of one jurisdiction are concerned with service levels in others, whether there should be a national standard in, say, local education.

Sinn: This discussion is very topical for Europe, but I have the impression that our American friends assume too much. They assume that the centralized Europe is already there and talk about the question of how it should efficiently be organized. We are not that far here in Europe even though yesterday the eleven-member countries of the common currency have been determined. Bernd Genser wanted to say something.

Bernd Genser, University of Konstanz: I want to take as a starting point the new proposal of the European Union for a unified value added tax in Europe, which includes identical VAT rates throughout Europe and a supranational distribution of VAT revenues according to national account statistics. This would clearly be a dramatic change in national tax autonomy and would also have important consequences for fiscal policy. The proposal resembles the current VAT system in Germany, where each "Land" is entitled to a certain share of VAT revenue, but the amount is determined by federal legislation. One important weakness of this revenue sharing system is that the subfederal governments finance a major part of their budgets from these funds but have no discretion about the amount of revenue from VAT. In particular, they cannot use VAT as a marginal source of funding public expenditures. In Germany, this is true for all the relevant taxes of the Länder. Although the German tax constitution only determines two federal duties: customs duties and royalties on state monopolies, all the other taxes that could be levied according to subfederal tax legislation have been centralized. Revenue sharing implies that subfederal governments face exogenous budget constraints and have no incentive to reduce their spending. The same would be true for national governments under the new Commission proposal. The other constitutional provision of financing subfederal budgets in Germany would be tax autonomy. But tax rates on mobile tax bases cannot be varied independently since tax bases flee to low tax regions and tax competition leads to another binding budget constraint. This characterizes the current situation in the European Union and tax competition is likely to increase in the Economic and

Monetary Union with shrinking transaction costs for tax arbitrage. What we should look for are tax systems that do not only support the preservation of decentralized tax autonomy on major tax bases but also limit harmful tax competition. A VAT system that seems to fulfill these objectives for the EU has been proposed by Keen and Smith. Their two-tier VAT consists of a unified VAT levied throughout the EU at the same rate and national retail sales taxes levied at country specific rates. Canada and the United States operate decentralized commodity taxes, although in the United States we only have sales taxes at the state level and no federal VAT. With respect to income taxes, Germany is again a federation without subfederal discretion, whereas Switzerland serves as an interesting example besides Canada and the United States. So I think that the most important tax policy task is to find a tax constitution that allows combining inframarginal fiscal funding by harmonized taxes and tax rates that are fixed by a federal or central authority, with marginal fiscal funding by autonomous taxes that open the efficient tax bases to decentralized units, too.

Peter Lewisch, University of Vienna: Let me approach the same set of issues from a somewhat different perspective. Let us consider again tax competition among states. I think the more philosophical theory of the state gives the right perspective: Competition among jurisdictions generates internal constraints, constraints that limit the power of the single government. These endogenously created constraints lead to a delegation of power downward to the individuals. Such competition has taken place in earlier centuries with respect to human rights. It did not end up in uniform bundles of rights offered by these jurisdictions, but in different sets of bundles; uniformity is not the necessary ultimate outcome. Competition among jurisdictions, therefore, is in fact a congenial institutional device to limit the power of governments. With regard to the more specific tax application, I think the case of Luxembourg provides a good example because it shows that the challenge for European Community law does not only consist in the need for a tax constitution *in abstracto*. We find ourselves in a specific status quo right now, and the problem is how do we leave the status quo and improve the situation if at all possible. And here, if Luxembourg is in the lucky position of being a tax haven for companies in Europe, why should it give up its position? It is always more beneficial to remain outside such a tax regime. And if the suggestion is then to tax or to punish Luxembourg for staying outside, how should that be done? There is no appropriate institution to allow for taxation. So again the appropriate institution would have to be implemented, but how? Again only by violating existing constitutional principles. If one has simply the idea of forcing Luxembourg into compliance with the "big community," one should be aware of the fact that this would require a change of existing constitutional rules, and, as long as Luxembourg is dissenting, such a change could only be realized by a violation of the pertinent constitutional framework.

Sinn: Yes, thank you. Well, I think we have to come to an end. However, I would like to ask our two speakers one last question. Namely, the question how much centralization would you think is necessary for Europe? Where should Europe go in this regard? Who wants to start?

Buchanan: I don't think I could dare try to give a comprehensive answer to that question. I think it is going to depend on the particulars of the situation. Again, as I said in relation to another context yesterday, how do you define discrimination, fiscal discrimination? It is much easier to say which way you are heading than it is to define it, and it is the same

here. It is much easier to say, for me at least, that a lot of the
existing thrust and development seem to me to be more in
the direction of granting too much authority to Brussels to
regularize and harmonize among the separate nation-states
than would be optimal from my perspective and from a
perspective of an effective competitive federalism. However,
it is easier to do that than it is to say what should be or what
shouldn't be. That would depend on the particulars of the
situation. It seems to me that it would not be a good idea
just allowing things to happen. It seems to me there has been
too much of that in the construction of the European Union
already. There has been a drift, and in a drift situation you
have got the bureaucracy doing a lot of things that they
shouldn't be allowed to do. It seems to me that it is time for
Europe to sit down and really try to develop a firm constitutional structure. To agree on a constitutional structure that
will do precisely what William Niskanen said, that will clear
these dividing lines, and unless that is done anything is
likely to happen. I don't see any real thrust toward that, but
I think it is very desirable that it be done.

Musgrave: Coordination can work in either of two ways.
One is to equalize, and the other is to permit differences but
to harmonize them so that distorting effects are avoided. So
I think that one of the central functions has to be to provide
an apparatus that makes it possible to harmonize while
maintaining differences, because otherwise competition will
force coordination by equalization. Differences will be permitted, with public services and redistributive activity
equalized at a minimum level. I am not arguing for centralization but against destructive competition, and this requires
some coordination among jurisdictions.

Day 5 (27 March 1998)

5.1

Morals, Politics, and Institutional Reform: Diagnosis and Prescription

James M. Buchanan

I Introduction

In earlier sessions of this seminar, Professor Musgrave and I laid out some elements of our visions of the public economy, of the political sector of activity, both in positive explanation-understanding-interpretations of how this sector operates and in a normative evaluation of this sector's operation against that which might be considered to be "best" within the limits of feasible attainment. In our planning for the organization of the whole series, we had designated this final session to cover, first, a diagnosis of the current state of affairs, both as we observe the public economy to operate and as we also observe public or citizenry attitudes toward such operation, and, second, some prescription for reform or improvement.

Within some limits, we have kept within our disciplinary boundaries. We have acted as political economists, which has allowed us legitimately to make the occasional forays into political science, political sociology, and political philosophy. For this final lecture, however, we must go beyond these boundaries. Almost by necessity, any diagnosis of socioeconomic-political order at the end of the century must also involve a moral-ethical dimension. We must become moral philosophers in the eighteenth-century meaning of this term.

In making such a statement, I am suggesting that the issues of current importance may not be centrally economic or political, at least in any direct sense. The issues may be moral, in important respects, although both economic and political elements may be relevant causal influences. Recognition of this fact does not imply that I plan to jump totally out of my professional limits and become a preacher. But such recognition does suggest that discussions of institutional reform must be focused on possible effects along moral dimensions rather than primarily along more familiar economic terrain.

How can the moral foundations of political order be restored? How can the institutions and agents of our politics come to command the respect that is necessary for effective functioning? How can some twentieth-first-century equivalent of "the idea of progress" that dominated nineteenth- and early twentieth-century thought be conceived, designed, and brought into reality? How can the blight of civil order wrought by our terrible twentieth century be erased? How can the civilization and culture of western Europe and America regain the confidence of its own participants?

Only in a limited way can political and economic reforms in institutional-constitutional structures be positively helpful in response to these critical questions. At best, or so it seems to me, institutional settings can be modified such as to facilitate the genuine transformation in behavior patterns that must occur.

I shall organize this lecture as follows: In sections II, III, and IV, below, I shall summarize three earlier and separate efforts that I have made at diagnosis. Each of these efforts was made in response to specific requests; they differ substantially, therefore, in their emphases. In section V, I combine the separate arguments into a general diagnostic criticism of existing political reality, as observed at the end of the century. In section VI, I assess prospects for melioration by reforms in the institutional structures of politics, that is, through effective constitutional change. The discussion in section VII centers on the metaphor of "social capital" that must be present in any tolerably acceptable moral order. In a concluding section VIII, a final assessment is offered, one that leaves open the central questions. I remain agnostic as to whether or not Western civic order can survive in anything like its traditional form.

II Markets, States, and the Extent of Morals

The title of this section is the one that I gave to a paper prepared for an American Economic Association meeting in early 1978 (Buchanan 1978). I was invited by Robert Solow to participate in a panel in which the separate speakers were asked, specifically, to discuss what each considered to be the most fundamental issues of social order.

I can summarize my argument, which surely remains as relevant in 1998 as it was in 1978. My starting point was the proposition that humans possess moral capacities that allow them to incorporate the interests of others than themselves as motivating forces in behavior, but that these capacities are limited along the dimensions that measure the number, locational proximity, and relationships of the others involved. A second proposition was that political interaction, by logical necessity, involves or includes all members of the relevant political community, in comparison and contrast with private interaction that reduces the direct relationship among parties to those that are voluntarily chosen, including the buyer-seller setting for the exchange nexus. From these propositions there follows, as a necessary corollary, the result that a person's moral capacities are more challenged in a political, or collective, interaction than in any voluntaristic relationship. By more challenged, I mean only that a person must make a more extensive "moral leap" if narrowly defined self-interest is to be somehow transcended. As an increasing share of social interaction has come to be politicized, and especially as such politicization has involved shifting of authority to more inclusive political communities, persons' moral capacities may become exhausted, at which margin behavioral reversion to opportunistic self-interest may manifest itself.

I suggested that this feature of modern politics is exhibited particularly when fiscal redistribution, in the form of tax-financed welfare transfers, is implemented through the authority of polities with large constituencies. Persons will tend, and increasingly so as the transfer sector expands, to behave in the narrow interests of their own perceived class, group, geographic district, profession, occupation, or industry. As a consequence, the modern welfare state, which might have remained viable either in smaller polities or at lower levels of transfer, may founder in the sense that demands for entitlementlike transfers may exceed the revenues that persons, as taxpayers, are willing to generate. Claimancy for transfers on the one hand, and resistance to taxation on the other, may be motivated more by targeted distributional objectives than by any generalized considerations for equity or justice. The observed fiscal crises in modern welfare democracies may be traceable in no small measure to the working out of these effects.

III Moral Anarchy, Moral Community, and Moral Order

The second, and related, effort on my part was stimulated by an invitation to visit Osaka, Japan, in 1981, under the auspices of the Suntory Foundation and to present a paper for an international forum entitled "Japan Speaks." Each speaker was explicitly asked to explore the question as to whether or not Japan could maintain its internal ethical cohesion as the level of economic well-being increased. Or was it inevitable and predictable that Japan would undergo its own "Americanization" in manners and morals?

I found it useful to set up and distinguish three ideal types or models, which I called "moral anarchy," "moral community," and "moral order." By the first, I referred to that behavioral manifestation which reflects the pursuit of narrowly defined and opportunistic self-interest on the part of all or a large share of persons in social interaction. In this stylized setting, persons generally treat other persons simply as parts of the natural world, so to speak, and exhibit no sense of reciprocal respect for other persons, as such.

In the second model or ideal type, as stylized persons, at least a large number treat others in the community as extensions of their own selves and behave as if the inclusive community is the relevant moral unit, whose interests are to be furthered. In this idealized model, there is no interpersonal conflict within communities. Conflict emerges only on the boundaries among separate moral communities.

The third ideal type, or model, requires perhaps somewhat more discussion. I take this model from F. A. Hayek, who made this set of attitudes an important requirement for what he called the "great society" (Hayek 1979). In a "moral order," persons do not treat the interests of others as their own (save for family members). But, on the other hand, neither do they treat others as moral outcasts, as in moral anarchy—that is, as a part of the natural world. In a moral order, other persons are recognized to be units of the human species and to exist as potential reciprocating partners in mutually beneficial interactions, in exchanges, broadly defined. The moral relationship between persons in this setting is one in which each person exhibits respect for and tolerance toward the other, and each adheres to rules that allow for generality in treatment, as opposed to opportunistic exploitation and discrimination. Note that the descriptive features of a moral order are those that are present in an effectively working market nexus, but note also that the same set of attitudes may be extended to collective interaction. The public or politicized sector of an economy in the idealized moral order is an extension of the exchange nexus to incorporate all members of the polity.

After setting up the three ideal types or stylized models of interaction, I then tried to classify differing societies by the mix among the three models. The Japan of the 1960s, 1970s, and early 1980s, the Japan for which "Japan, Inc." retained considerable empirical relevance, embodied more of the features of moral community than did the societies of the United States or western Europe. These latter societies, in part because of historical traditions, seemed to me to embody more elements of a moral order, in some relative sense, than Japan. My precautionary warning was that Japan might be more vulnerable to lapses into moral anarchy because of the absence of historical traditions that had allowed for the slow development of attitudes described under the moral order rubric. I did not, however, neglect to point out that all modern societies, Eastern and Western, face continuing threats to their moral cohesion by increasing reversion toward moral anarchy by more and more members of their political communities.

Retrospectively considered, my 1981 argument (Buchanan 1981) may be interpreted as an advocacy of the norms of classical liberalism, norms that dictate the superior efficacy of the moral stance described by the "moral order" as the ideal type. I sensed the dangers of "moral anarchy" everywhere, and I did not reckon on any emergence of genuine "moral community" anywhere, with either its potentially desirable or undesirable features. As related to the earlier argument about moral capacities, the point was made that the post–World War II expansions in the relative size of the public sector of national economies must surely have contributed to an erosion of moral standards, thereby making "moral anarchy" increasingly descriptive as a model of social interaction.

IV Transcending Genetic Limits

My third, and again related, effort at generalized diagnosis was made in 1997, when I was invited by an Italian sponsor to prepare a lecture on "Humankind at the Beginning of the Third Millennium." Much had happened in the history of the decade and a half since the Japanese lecture. The great revolutions of 1989–1991 occurred, which none of us, as political economists, political scientists, or political philosophers, had predicted.

Is Francis Fukuyama correct in suggesting that the long dialectic struggle between individualism and collectivism has ended, and that, henceforth, political economies will be increasingly organized on market principles, and that polities will evolve into liberal democracies (Fukuyama 1992)? It seemed useful to look at this question in terms of the three models introduced in the earlier Japanese paper, the models of moral anarchy, moral community, and moral order. What the collapse of communism, and the end of socialist ideology, accomplished was a weakening of those elements of moral community that made persons incorporate the interests of the nation-state, the national collectivity, into their own psyches. Beyond the Cold War, beyond the presence of the external enemy, what is the raison d'etre of the nation-state, as it exists? Simple honesty forces us to acknowledge, in 1998, that little other than history itself ties citizens of national political communities together. Collectivities define themselves, as coherent entities that command personal loyalties, by their enemies. And who is the enemy in 1998? (Modern Israel stands as a notable exception to the generalization here.)

This overall diagnosis led me, in the 1997 lecture, to suggest that humankind's greatest challenge at the end of the century was to prevent the reemergence of tribal conflict, waged among and between those "natural" collectivities that can command personal loyalties at some deep level that may bear little relationship to political reality. I suggested that prospective reforms might be made by the deliberate organization of federalized structures that embody devolution of authority to units that are sufficiently small to command personal allegiance but that, at the same time, do not evoke tribal urges, defined broadly to include those based on ethnic, racial, or religious boundaries.

(Let me digress briefly at this point to suggest that Europe offers a partial exception to the generalization here. "Europe as an idea," that is, as a collective unit that transcends traditional national limits, has the potential to command at least a modicum of personal commitment, at least for some period, and particularly if it is conceived by Europeans themselves as a "superior" socioeconomic-cultural entity, as compared with the "primitive" societies of America, Eastern Europe, and Asia.)

In my 1997 assessment (Buchanan 1997), which I share in 1998, I am less sanguine about the potential viability of the classical liberal, post-Enlightenment, ideal for social order than might have been implied in my earlier diagnoses. Perhaps I have been influenced by the failure of the great revolutions of 1989–1991 to have exerted much demonstrable influence on Western politics, and perhaps also by the apparent strength in the arguments of modern communitarian critics. Is a society that is held together only by some mutuality of respect among citizens who interact within a functioning rule of law acceptable, even as an ideal, or as some ultimate objective for political policy? This question remains even if we could imagine a setting where governments again regain confidence that its actions are limited to those that translate the demands of citizens for commonly shared goods and services.

Classical Rome does not offer us encouragement here. Rome did provide law and order; it failed, in part, because it did not go beyond this and offer some transcendent ideal—whether religious, racial, or otherwise—that could command and capture personal attention. Aided and abetted by the observed corruption of its political agents, Rome proved vulnerable both to the tribal hordes and to the new religion that promised personal salvation.

V The Limits of Moral Order

An inclusive and generalized diagnosis of social order at the century's end may be readily translated into the three stylized models or ideal types introduced earlier. The plaint of the modern communitarians is well directed in the sense that, empirically, there does seem to exist, on the part of many persons, a genuine desire to belong to, to be part of, some community larger than themselves and their own family unit. This longing is perhaps accentuated by the decline in the importance of the extended family and its replacement by the welfare state.

It has been well over a century since Nietzsche proclaimed the death of God, and this century has witnessed the death of its putative replacement in the nation-state. What is to be and to become the symbol of community? There seems to be little, if any, behavioral motivation in anything that might be called "moral community," as such. (Contrast 1998 with 1898 in this respect alone. In 1898, the moral force of "empire" drove leaders such as Cecil Rhodes to action, over and beyond, even if consistent with, self-interest.) Who among us, as citizens of Western nations, is likely to think much, if at all, about the "national interest," as we go about making our ordinary day-to-day choices, either in private or public capacities?

In the classical liberal ideal, of course, this decline in the motivating force of moral community is a praiseworthy feature of modernity. To the extent that persons lose their sense of self-identity defined in ethnic, racial, national, or religious terms, to be replaced by some generalized sense of membership in the human community, progress toward the post-Enlightenment ideal has been made. Or, to put the argument in terms of the three models, to the extent that the motivating force of moral community is effectively replaced by that of moral order, the world becomes a better place. The critical question is, however, whether any such replacement has taken, is taking, place and in what degree. Does it not seem more likely that the demise in moral community, and especially as this tends to constrain behavioral excesses, is accompanied by a shift toward moral anarchy?

It is important to define terms carefully here. Moral anarchy, as a generalized behavioral attitude, does not necessarily embody "immoral action" in any particular setting. In politics in particular, moral anarchy involves nothing more than the ordinary pursuit of private or group interest at the acknowledged cost of "public" interest, with the latter defined as the inclusion of all relevant political externalities. Ordinary understanding does not label as "immoral" the efforts of, say, a group to secure differentially favorable tax treatment. Moral anarchy describes the attitude in which there is no sense of commonality among persons, and hence no sense of reciprocation that sets up human interaction as something apart from interaction with nature.

Political economy, from its classical origins in the eighteenth century, has recognized that moral anarchy may indeed describe much human behavior. And the great discovery of the classical economists was the recognition that markets may work to channel such behavior toward mutually beneficial ends, provided that property and personal rights are well defined and enforced and that the laws against force and fraud are in place. Even in market regimes, however, constraints on opportunistic behavior, within the strict limits of law, may be necessary for any approximation toward reaching the classical ideal. Absent any elements of moral order, externalities in market dealings might simply be too pervasive to generate even tolerable efficiency in resource use. And, of course, in politics all choices necessarily embody externalities, in the sense that "all others" are always affected by the choices that are made.

At its worst, however, moral anarchy is to be preferred over moral community in its most virulent form, where membership is defined by belief in revealed truth. In such a setting, behavior, whether private or collective, extends beyond any economically motivated effort at mutual exploitation to effort aimed at destruction, even at the expense of economic interest. The zealot murders in the name of truth, as revealed.

The challenge is to prevent the leap into the intolerance of moral community while somehow restoring some semblance of civil community, as summarized under the rubric of moral order. But sober assessment suggests that the twenty-first century will not be ushered in with some rediscovered ethic of mutual tolerance. Nor will one set of putative moral virtues emerge to command universal assent. John Rawls recognized the plight of modernity when he launched his plea for attainment of the minimal consensus necessary for political peace and justice, minimal consensus even in the face of divergent supreme values (Rawls 1993).

VI Institutional Reform

By suggesting that observed behavior, both in private and public choice, is not sufficiently motivated by the moral norms that would be necessary to sustain something like post-Enlightenment liberal society, I am implying that the institutional structure within which such behavior takes place is failing. Observed opportunistic behavior, both in markets and in politics, suggests an absence of moral constraints. Trust in markets seems everywhere replaced by threat of litigation, and trust in politics can scarcely be sustained in the face of near-total corruption.

Two separate conclusions may be drawn from this gloomy assessment of socioeconomic-political order. The first is defeatist and falls back on an argument to the effect that the whole Enlightenment edifice was, from the start and for two centuries, a romantic dream that must now be viewed only as philosophic fiction. (See Gray 1995.) The second conclusion, which I feel myself morally obligated to share, remains meliorist in its claim that properly designed institutional-constitutional change can move behavior at least some direction toward the classical liberal set of minimal standards that seem necessary.

One direction for constructive reform seems clear. Much of the moral rot that we observe, in both private and public behavior, is traceable to the exaggerated size of the public sector relative to the total economy. If this sector could be reduced to a proportionate share roughly equivalent to that which described the state at midcentury, much good would be done. We must acknowledge that the bloated welfare-transfer state that we now live with was allowed to grow in the shadow of the Cold War over the half-century and without attention to its own external diseconomies. Belatedly, in the 1990s, reforms everywhere have been initiated that are aimed at reducing the relative weight of the public sector overall, or at least reducing its rate of growth. These reforms proceed under varying names—privatization, devolution, subsidiarity, decentralization—some of which have been discussed in earlier sessions.

At this point, I must shift the focus of my argument. I have suggested variously that the fundamental issues facing modern societies are *moral,* and that institutional reforms have an influence in changing attitudes and patterns of behavior. Specifically, I have suggested that a major reduction in the relative size of the public sector of social interaction might accomplish at least some of the transformation that is needed. But have I done anything more than criticize, personally, the decisions that have been made, through broadly democratic political processes? Until and unless I can also demonstrate that the relative size of the public sector has been generated through a biased decision process, there might seem to be little space for agreed-on reform.

Here I suggest that an argument from standard economic efficiency can be adduced that will show that the size of the collectivized section of the modern economy is too large. This argument, standing alone, implies that more economic value may be generated by institutional-constitutional change aimed at constraining the collectivized sector, quite apart from any complementary effects on the moral-ethical attitudes that might emerge. At this point, the economics and the ethics of the argument merge into one.

The Public as Commons

It is useful to think of the inclusive public economy in the familiar metaphor of the commons, with the tragic dissipation of potential value due to overuse of a resource. In the classic illustration, recall that each and every decision to use the commons, as made by the separate choosers (e.g., to add additional cattle to graze on the common pasture), is itself privately separately rational in the sense that expected benefits exceed or are equal to expected costs. But, because each user's action generates external diseconomies on all other users, in the final equilibrium the full value of the common resource may, in the limit, be destroyed. Think of each separate public choice, made by a dominant majority coalition, which assesses its own benefits against its own costs. The externalities imposed on persons outside the co-alition are neglected. As electoral rotation shifts the makeup of majority coalitions, the whole set of public choices be-comes fully analogous to those choices made by separate users to apply resources to the commons. In the public economy, the commons is the tax base from which all collective goods must be financed. The public sector will be overextended as measured against standard efficiency criteria (Tullock 1959; Buchanan and Tullock 1962; Buchanan and di Pierro 1969). Over some relevant range, a reduction in the relative size of the public or collectivized sector of the economy will generate an increase in aggregate economic value.

But how can the relative size of the public sector be reduced? Suppose that there is a generalized recognition that the public sector is too large, and suppose, further, that this recognition prompts general approval of a constitutional rule that dictates an aggregate upper bound (say, at 25 percent of GDP). What public projects or proposals are to be excluded? Any selective or arbitrary reduction will leave projects undone that promise to yield net positive value to members of potential majority coalitions. This value shortfall will set off investments in efforts to capture decision authority through membership in emergent new coalitions. Majoritarian rent seeking (Buchanan 1995) will take place, and resources devoted to this purpose may "eat up" most if not all of the value increment that is promised by the constitutionally imposed constraint on public-sector size.

Generality

A complementary constitutional requirement that dictates generality, both in the imposition of taxes and the provision of public goods benefits (including cash transfers), can do much to reduce, and perhaps dramatically, the incentives for majoritarian rent seeking. If overt discrimination both in the exaction of taxes and the distribution of benefits is ruled out-of-bounds for ordinary politics, majority rule may work with tolerable effectiveness. As noted in an earlier lecture, majority coalitions will differ in their revealed preferences along some relevant dimensions of fiscal adjustment, but the potential gains from explicit fiscal exploitation will be largely if not completely eliminated.

VII Social Capital

The discussion in the preceding section summarizes practicable institutional-constitutional change that might be introduced that would have the indirect effect of affecting the morality of both private and public behavior. But the question remains: Would such institutional-constitutional reform itself be sufficient? Even with a public sector reduced, to, say, one-half its current relative size in most Western nations, and even if this sector should be restricted to nondiscriminatory action, will persons draw back from mutually destructive opportunistic behavior in markets and in politics? Will they adopt attitudes of honesty and reciprocal respect, one for another? Will reform, in itself, generate a socioeconomic-political order that resembles the classical liberal ideal?

As I have already suggested, I am not optimistic as I try to answer my own questions here. This terrible century has done much more than bear witness to the tragic failures of collectivist controls over personal lives. In the processes of those failed experiments, valuable social capital was allowed to depreciate, capital that was represented in personal attitudes of independence, obeying laws, self-reliance, hard work, self-confidence, a sense of permanence, trust, mutual respect, and tolerance. This capital has been eroded only to be replaced by attitudes that embody irresponsibility, dependency, differential exploitation, opportunistic advantage seeking, short-run hedonism, legal trimming, litigation, mistrust, and intolerance, especially for the "politically incorrect." The potential gains from collective action might be relatively easy to capture in an environment described by the presence of the first set of attitudes. But any such gains from collective action may be jeopardized in the environment we witness at the turn of the century. Until and unless persons, as citizens, can trust each other, as citizens and as agents, neither the economy nor the polity can function effectively.

The moral order that describes the classical liberal ideal may have been within the possible at the beginning of the century. Whether it is within the possible at century's end seems much more problematic. The economists' concept of capital, at least as metaphor, is helpful in understanding. Capital is stored-up value, yielding a stream of returns over a whole sequence of periods. And, importantly, capital creation is itself a time-consuming project; capital is created over time by abstinence. Capital, once brought into existence, may be quickly destroyed, but it cannot be restored over a short time span. "Social capital," as reflected in both behavioral norms and public attitudes, has surely been eroded over the century. Quite apart from the institutional transformation needed to provide the incentives for renewal here, there must emerge, in parallel, some rebirth of spirit, some sense of shared purpose, in the society of freely choosing citizens. Ronald Reagan's evocation of the American Puritans' promise of a "shining city on a hill" must become more than a romantic dream.

VIII Conclusion

Perhaps I should end this lecture with that rhetorical flourish. I have offered both diagnosis and prescription, which was my initial assignment. But I finish on a false note if I leave any impression that the new century could possibly commence with a vibrant international community of separate nation-states, each competing with others in orderly markets and each described internally by a stable and secure sociopolitical order, in which persons retain liberties of personal choice over wide ranges of behavior, and in which governments act, everywhere, as instruments of citizens rather than as exploiting agents for rent-seeking coalitions.

The century will not commence with such a description, nor will the citizenries of several nation-states employ that description in the images of social order that motivate behavior, private or public. By contrast, the century will commence with bloated public sectors, with governments faced with open-ended entitlement claims and unable to secure tax revenues sufficient to meet such claims, or even to finance minimally needed infrastructures. Political agents will not command public confidence and respect and such absence will, in its turn, generate moral depravity in the agents in political authority, due both to internal motivation and to the self-selection process.

To me, there seems to be no discernible spark of moral-ethical renewal. (I recall that, many decades past, there was a movement that called itself "moral rearmament." Where is the current equivalent?) Perhaps the depravity signaled by the latest Clinton scandals will ultimately generate such moral revulsion as to set off a reversal of the historical path toward moral decline. Robert Fogel, a distinguished economic historian and Nobel laureate, whose ideas deserve some attention, is openly predicting that we are on the verge of a period of great religious upheaval. Perhaps. Western societies, especially, seem to be vulnerable to movements that will shift public sights to "larger things," to "other worlds." But such movements can spell disaster as readily as stability and uplift. On the other hand, tribal anarchy threatens as the alternative in the continued absence of some reawakening.

But lest we get overly pessimistic about where we are and where we may be headed, let me call attention to where we have been. Yes, overall, it has been a terrible century. But imagine yourself transported back a mere quarter century, to 1973, before there were even inklings that the Cold War was near its close. We could never have predicted (and we did not) that, by 1998, the Cold War would have been ended peaceably and that, almost everywhere, persons' liberties would have increased along with their economic well-being. Who knows, we may now be overlooking prospects for a better socioeconomic-political world of nation-states than any of us can now describe, even in our dreams.

5.2   Response

Richard A. Musgrave

This is not the usual kind of paper that is discussed at an economics seminar. The efficiency of morals (or is it the morality of efficiency?) has not been a standard topic in economics texts, not even in those on public finance. However, I accept the challenge and will follow in its spirit. In contrast to my previous paper, however, I do disagree with much of Professor Buchanan's argument, including his diagnosis of the welfare state and its future. The welfare state and expanding budgets, so he argues, have demoralized society and by cutting them, morality will be restored. I wonder.

I   The Three Models

I begin with the three types of moral order around which the paper is built. They are defined in terms of how people behave toward each other, not necessarily the only criterion, but alright for this purpose. The first model is that of "moral anarchy," where people engage in "opportunistic self-interested behavior" with no sense of reciprocal respect. The second is that of "moral community," where individuals consider others as extensions of themselves, making the inclusive community the relevant moral unit. The third is the "moral order," where people respect others and recognize their existence as partners in mutually beneficial enterprises, conducted under generally applicable rules. This condition is met by the market and also by cooperation in the provision of public goods. He then ranks the three, not explicitly, but implicitly as I read from his argument. Anarchy is not nice, as we all agree, and community is better but dangerous, leaving the market as best of all. This formulation troubles me in various ways.

Professor Buchanan, I think, falls into the trap of moving from the role of ideal types as reflections of "pure" states, as Weber meant them, to viewing them as states of affairs among which we must choose. "Ideal" in Weber's sense does not mean "desirable" or available. I do not have to choose between Jean Jacques Rousseau and Friedrich von Hayek , nor is there any need for me to do so. Community may turn into terror but even if it does not, my choice between listening to music or reading a book should be my private affair only. At the same time, I do not buy Buchanan's moral order in its pure form. Relating to the well-being of others only in the context of mutually profitable exchange seems to me amoral at best. It surely does not meet the essential tradition of Western civilization, as expressed in John's parable of the Good Samaritan, in Luke's golden rule, or in Kant's categorical imperative. My choice, and I will refer to it here as the "good society," is one that combines the self-interest-based principle of the market as an efficient institution with justice and communal concern for others as its moral input. This recognizes that the market resolves one major aspect of social relations but by no means all of them. Some of the most important problems, including that of distribution, are indeed of a different kind. If economists wish to become moral philosophers, they must therefore step beyond the Pareto restraint. Half the time, I think that Professor Buchanan agrees with much of this, but then I wonder when I find him embracing Hayek's "great society" as *the* goal.

II A Disastrous Century?

Placing our own time in that spectrum, the paper offers what is indeed a gloomy assessment of the Western world. It speaks of the "blight on civil order wrought by our terrible twentieth century," of the "near total corruption of politics," of "moral rot," of "depravity," and so forth. Is the state of our civilization really that bad and has the record of this century been that terrible?

The twentieth century has been marked by two terrible wars, made more deadly than those of the past by the advancing technology of destruction, but morally not necessarily worse than the Crusades or the Thirty Years' War of the Middle Ages. It is true that here have been unthinkable episodes of brutality, such as the Stalinist terror and the Holocaust. But many of these terrible events occurred during the first half of the century, and I would suggest that the second half has been a success. There have been no major wars, the Soviet system ran its course, nuclear war has been contained, and the advent of the European Union bodes well for a peaceful future.

Looking at Germany, it may well be argued that the second half of this century has been the best since the golden age of Goethe, Herder, Kant, and Schiller (cited in alphabetical order!). The firm basis for a democratic society has been laid, and the extensive aid given to the new Länder after reunification has also been an exercise in social morality that should be allowed for.

Even in the United States—whose record, I take it, Professor Buchanan finds especially distressing—there is much that should go on the credit side of the ledger. The taming of unbridled capitalism and the injection of social responsibility that began with the New Deal, was a step forward, and so was the introduction of health insurance in the sixties. Socializing the capitalist system (as distinct from turning it into socialism as the paper suggests!) was needed for its own survival and for building a good society. Most important, and not mentioned by Professor Buchanan, there has been a revolutionary change in the status of black people, from the Supreme Court ruling on school segregation in 1954 to the banning of job discrimination in 1964 and the civil rights movement of that decade. Much remains to be done but these attainments, the first real progress since the Civil War in extending human rights across color lines was, as I see it, an enormous gain in public morality. This alone, not to mention gains in the status of women and of other minorities, would make me hesitant to write off this century as a terrible one. Public mores on what is right and what is wrong in race relations took a leap to the better. Not all went well, to be sure, and much remains to be done. Along with others, I find many things to complain about, for example, the intolerance of political correctness, abuse of welfare rights, disrespect of government, and so forth. But the past also had its faults. Looking back at the fifties, we have the McCarthy days, and going back a further three centuries, we recall that pious Pilgrims burned their witches. Professor Buchanan, I think, paints too gloomy a picture of how we have done.

I will not turn this discussion into an intramural debate about the state of the States, but would add this observation. There *is* much that needs to be done to improve our federal government and the respect in which it is held, with reform of campaign financing, not of voting rules the most urgent step. Reforms are needed, but matters have not been helped by the continuous pounding given to government by Professor Buchanan and other critics, thereby adding to the very disrespect for government that they seek to reduce. I think this is unfortunate. The role of the intellectual in this TV age is no longer what it was when candlelights were in use, and intellectual leaders should be aware of that and act responsibly.

III The Tragedy of the Samaritan

I now turn to more specific observations regarding the nexus between the economy and social morals, including its bearing on the future of the welfare state.

Professor Buchanan, now a quarter of a century ago, published a paper entitled "The Samaritan's Dilemma " (Buchanan 1975b). I then found the message deeply disturbing and invited him to present it to my class, an event that my Harvard students and I remember well. The central message—I would call it "The Samaritan's Tragedy," rather than "Dilemma"—was that in trying to do good (10 Luke, 25–27), he may create bad. Moral hazard, as economists strangely call it (or should it be immoral hazard?), then suggests that the Samaritan had better withdraw his helping hand. I thought this to be an unsettling message, one that stabs at the heart of Western morality and its traditions and am disturbed to find it reappearing in today's lecture, but there it is.

There is, to be sure, a difference between helping a robber's victim, as did the Samaritan, and giving public support
to people who prefer relief to work. But reality falls in
between, and policy must address real situations. The good
society calls for leaning toward help where needed or, better
still, creating institutions wherever possible that preclude
such need. Nor should we be too surprised when those
helped sleep an hour later. Income effects may outweigh
substitution effects at the bottom of the scale, just as the
opposite may hold in response to taxation at the upper end.

IV Diagnosis and Cure

Confronted with what Professor Buchanan considers to be
the collapse of moral society, he finds that "much of the rot
is to be attributed to the rise of the public sector;" and, based
on that diagnosis, his cure is to cut it back. I find both
diagnosis and cure unconvincing.

His vision of moral collapse (including not only the
United States, but the whole Western world!) is overly pessimistic, as suggested before, and his assessment of public
sector growth as *the* causal factor is surely overdrawn. Just
what damage is it that we are asked to consider? Is it that
availability of a social safety net has weakened work effort,
that social insurance has reduced saving, and that taxation
has depressed work incentives? While there is a bit of truth
in each of these, the effects have been spotty and need to be
balanced against the gains to civilized and productive living
that the public sector has rendered, including improved
education and public health. As wealth and the amenities of
civilized government improve, some of the puritan virtues
may be lost. But must people really be kept poor and scared
to remain virtuous? And is it not true that Americans in
particular work more, not less, to partake in the "good" life?

And may not excessive concern with material welfare, to the neglect of other things, be part of our problem?

There are other bads that worry Professor Buchanan (as they do me) such as a decline in civility, reduced trust in business transactions, intolerance and a reduced faith that we, as a society, are on the right track. Not all is well, but it is hard to blame the rise of the public sector for all these ills. Structural change along with the growth in our market economy produced problems not readily resolvable by the puritan virtues of self-reliance and hard work. People lost the security of their farms, and employment has become less stable. The vagaries of the business cycle and changing markets have exceeded those of the weather, family bonds have declined as the production unit has changed, and uncertainties have increased. Thus there has been a growing need for new institutions to provide support. In these and other respects, the rise of the public sector has been a responding rather than an initiating factor, and if it was, removal of the response will not restore bliss.

Expansion of the public sector, therefore, is not just a fluke, a technical defect that can be fixed like simply changing a fouled-up spark plug. More basically, it reflects changing needs and, with the rise of popular democracy, changing coalitions and wishes of the public. Schumpeter feared that this public, by progressive taxation, would kill enterprise before the bliss of unlimited plenty was reached, and Professor Buchanan similarly fears that discriminatory voting will become increasingly destructive of moral society. I think these projections are too Hegelian and expect the West to survive.

Turning now to the cure, the focus, as developed in Professor Buchanan's first paper and restated here, is on the damage done by discriminating coalitions, a damage to be prevented by imposing a domain of nondiscrimination. That strategy, though not my top priority for reform, will reduce arbitrary discrimination, which is good. But, as I mentioned in my earlier comment, care must be taken not also to bar desired differentiation. A generality rule will keep some pork-barrel roads from passing, roads that do not serve the general interest, but may it not also bar a road needed as a link in a highway system? Providing equal road footage per square mile throughout the country would be truly nondis-criminatory but not very efficient, as would providing see-ing-eye dogs to the seeing and blind alike.

Similar concerns arise when the rule of generality is ap-plied to transfer systems. While useful in barring uncalled for and special-interest benefits, requiring benefits to be paid to all, whether needed or not, is expensive. The proposed approach to redistribution via a proportional tax-financed demogrant will swell the budget and, more important, leave out justified differentiation via higher bracket rates at the upper end of the scale. Requiring uniformity will check nuisance discrimination, but it also interferes with needed differentiation. Social problems are complex, and simple rules, elegant though they may seem, should be viewed with suspicion. Equal treatment of equals is a worthy pursuit, a goal for which my generation of tax reformers has battled over the decades. But appropriate differentiation among unequals, though more difficult to define, is also a worthy goal.

V Conclusion

One of my themes has been that the market, efficient and helpful as it is, does not by itself constitute a moral order. The vision of a moral order, based on self-interest only, is incongruous. The very concept of a moral and good society involves individuals in their relation to others, and that relation to be moral cannot be based only on self-interest or expediency. Respect for others is basic but self-interest, while useful in its place, is not enough. That shining city on the hill (5 Matthew, 14) to which Professor Buchanan, along with Ronald Reagan, hopes to return, will have to include government buildings as well as shopping plazas.

In conclusion, I return to the paper's three models, none of which I find acceptable. The anarchic state, neither efficient nor pretty, is out. The communal state is too intrusive on individual liberty where not needed and is also too dangerous. The third model, which Jim prefers and calls the "moral state," I find useful as a device to deal efficiently with what can be dealt with in that fashion, but insufficient by itself. It leaves out the essentially moral part of what I view as the moral state, that is, its mutual concern outside the Paretian orbit.

John Locke, by taking the entitlement to earnings as given by divine law, could fold morality into the market mode; so could Adam Smith in his *Wealth of Nations,* qualified, however, by the mysterious impartial spectator who roams the pages of his *Theory of Moral Sentiments.* Modern society can no longer take the Lockean view. Justice in distribution is not predetermined by natural law but must be faced by the moral state; and the Age of Enlightenment, where what had to be determined could be determined by pure reason, no longer holds. Distributive justice has to be confronted, and that need is not met by adding a bit, say one third, of Professor Buchanan's second model to his third. Rather, it calls for a distinct, make it the fourth, model, where individuals as citizens of their community share common obligations and do so on a daily basis, including their conduct of the public sector.

5.3   Discussion

Sinn: Thank you very much for this very concise statement. Now we have a discussion. Who wants to start? William Niskanen.

William Niskanen, Cato Institute: What type of institutional arrangements do we need to assure time consistency? In other words, how do we prevent each generation from treating the future as a commons?

Musgrave: Insofar as social security is concerned, you do want a funded system to sustain it as population ages, or else there should be current finance with benefits indexed to change with per capita average earnings net of contributions. I agree that equity across generations is not something that the market can handle, so government is needed.

Peter Bernholz, University of Basel: James Buchanan, your broad and sweeping vision has certainly extended our understanding and that is the positive side. On the other hand, I think it has left out some of the pressing bread-and-butter problems of the welfare state that we are faced with in Europe. I think that this point is also very important for us to understand and to make a decision between the point of view you take and Richard Musgrave takes. Namely, the question is whether the present welfare state, especially in western Europe, is maintainable or not.

But before I turn to that let me respond critically to one of your arguments. You have pointed out that the overextended welfare state erodes morality. I can agree with this position. But is it not also true that the developing capitalism has destroyed what you call a communitarian morality? It has to destroy it. Therefore, I have never believed that relevant characteristics of Confucianism or Shintoism would resist the onslaught of capitalism. It has destroyed the big family in the West, and we have to agree that the destruction of the big family as a supporting device brought about, if not necessitated, some development of the welfare state. Schumpeter pointed out already in his *Capitalism, Socialism and Democracy* (Schumpeter 1942) that the capitalistic system, because it is so creative and evolves with ever new innovations, is also a destructive process. It destroys, as he thought, also the moral foundations of society. Although I have some doubts about this, I think we have to take it into account.

The other question is, of course, whether the present European welfare state is maintainable? I think—at least since 1980—that it is not maintainable. I agree that a capitalist system is probably the only system that is able to carry the burden of a limited welfare state, and I have just pointed out that we probably need to limit the welfare state. I have done some empirical work, as have others; for instance, Tanzi and Schuhknecht showed only recently in a World Bank study that the higher the percentage of government expenditures in GDP, the lower is the growth rate. We have also done empirical work that shows that the longer the undisturbed age of democracy in the Olson sense, the lower the growth rate.

A considerably lower growth rate usually leads to unemployment as presently seen in western Europe, and this makes the present welfare state unaffordable. Furthermore, we have to consider the overextension of the old age pension system. According to the Wissenschaftliche Beirat of the German Economics Ministry in its recent study, the present system is also not maintainable. Of course this doesn't mean that we cannot have reforms, cutting it back to a maintainable dimension.

Now I would argue, however, James Buchanan, that there are forces at work to turn things around because the welfare state is going to enter a crisis. Given the right ideas, the crisis itself may help to bring about the turnaround. We have already seen such a turnaround in New Zealand, where the extended welfare state was in part based on agriculture that was especially weak. We have seen turnarounds in Britain and in the United States, and also a small, but obviously successful one, in the Netherlands. If one looks at those countries one can observe higher growth rates and receding unemployment.

Sinn: Yes, thank you. Joself Falkinger.

Josef Falkinger, University of Regensburg: I want to extend Professor Musgrave's criticism. Professor Buchanan argued that the moral capacity has been exhausted and people have become more opportunistic, and that this opportunistic behavior is an increasing function of the size of the public sector. I am not convinced by this argument. Do you really think, for instance, that people in China, say in the eighties, were more egoistic than an average citizen of the United States? I think we should not forget that, after all, a market economy is a system based on the idea of self-interest, that egoistic behavior is rewarded and attachment to ethical principles is punished. So we should not be surprised if people learn to pursue their self-interest, because this is the strategy that leads to success. I think the remedy must be to ask ourselves how we can modify the institutions of market economies so that not only the pursuit of self-interest but also fair behavior are rewarded and not penalized. Here lies the real reason for those findings. I think as economists, we tend to forget about this. If I remember correctly, this was also the worry of Adam Smith who feared that the market system, while being efficient, would induce people to forget their sense of duty and their feeling of fellowship. This was one of the reasons why Adam Smith thought that there should be a state as a counterforce to the market institutions that induce egoistic behavior.

Sinn: I think this is important. We should give Jim Buchanan the possibility to answer because it is not entirely clear what moral behavior really is. Is it moral behavior in the sense of altruism, or is it moral behavior in the sense that one simply respects others' property rights? James Buchanan, what is your definition of moral behavior?

Buchanan: Well, I will go back to Adam Smith. I am glad that you have brought Adam Smith in because his whole structure was built on acceptability of a set of laws and institutions and—he would have added, I am sure (and he did implicitly add)—a set of behavioral norms in which people do have mutual respect. He has been accused of being very provincial and talking about eighteenth-century Scotland, which of course he was, but that did embody a certain moral cement that people have in terms of this mutuality of respect. It is separate from altruism. It is, in fact, not that people need to be concerned in an altruistic way with others. But the functioning of a market order requires that people carry around with them this kind of sense of fairness in dealings. You can't necessarily fully enforce that through a law. I have debated this for a long time with some of my colleagues and others. It is argued by some people that all you need is an effective set of legal institutions to prohibit certain types of behavior. I don't think you could ever have a market work like that. I think that the market would fall down tomorrow if, in fact, people went strictly only by what is illegal and what is not illegal. You could never have enough law to enforce a market order. I think a market order critically depends on this sort of behavior that I exemplified in a moral order. In a market left alone, as modern Russia now indicates, you get all sorts of criminality and everything else if you just have short-run opportunistic behavior. That is not what I am concerned with. But you do have to make a distinction between pursuing self interest within the confines of moral laws of mutuality of respect of persons with whom you are dealing and a market operating just open-ended. In response to some of the other points, I agree with Peter Bernholz. Unbridled capitalism—in a sense even capitalism that satisfies some of the requirements that I set for a moral order—tends to undermine community. There is no way we are really going to resolve that conflict. It is going to be there. In response to William Niskanen's point, the question he raised is precisely the reason that I have been strongly supportive for decades of a balanced budget amendment. Governments can't be allowed to mortgage futures by spending more than they take in and putting the burden off to people. The funding of social security is one aspect of that.

Musgrave: James Buchanan mentioned Adam Smith, and I share his admiration. As with Wicksell, this is another point where we overlap, but I would urge people not only to read *The Wealth of Nations* but also *The Theory of Moral Sentiments*, where there is that impartial observer who roams the marketplace and reminds people that they ought to have a conscience.

Sinn: I would like to insist on this issue to make clear what you really mean. There is the communitarian moral, as in the Asian countries and, maybe a little bit, in Germany, and there is the individualistic moral. You prefer the latter. But do you prefer it because the market can't work without it, or is there a more fundamental reason?

Buchanan: Well, it is not a question of preferring. I think it is a question of what is necessary. Let me just go back to Hayek again and trace through some of Hayek's argument. Hayek argued that we never would have got into what he called the great society, that is the modern society, without this leap into moral order. He argued that we don't understand how we got there really. We shifted out of the medieval manor village, in which people associated with other people in this very localized tribal setting, in which you separate out who is a member of your group and who is the enemy and you kill the enemy. I have been listening to tapes of the Old Testament, and it is impressive how the early Israelites were forming a national community. They were forming community in the sense that you kill the enemy. Now Hayek's point is that the leap into moral order was accomplished when people began to recognize that they might trade with someone who was not a member of their moral community at all, someone from the other village. Adam Smith made this point—no dog exchanges a bone with another dog. In trade, you don't treat another person like an animal, as you would in a moral anarchy. You trade in a way that involves some sort of recognition of mutuality of respect. You accomplish an exchange process and from that arises specialization, a buildup in structure. And we do carry around with us, as Hayek says, a code of conduct, manners, orderly behavior, which every one of us accepts. The market won't work, unless we do. It's hard to imagine a market of any complexity at all working at the level of morals that would characterize the behavior of the hawker at the street carnival. None of us expect the hawker at the street carnival to be straightforward in his dealings. We expect to be fraudulently exploited in that context. And you can't generalize that sort of behavior at all. You have to have this mutuality of respect, and that is what is involved in what might be called the morality of the marketplace, the minimum morality of the marketplace, so to speak.

Sinn: So I interpret this as being a purely instrumental definition of morality. It's not the moral as such that has its value; it has its value indirectly because it makes exchange possible, and if one finds other ways of interaction between people, then you wouldn't mind a communitarian moral.

Buchanan: The argument I just gave could be interpreted to be instrumental, but I also think it has other more basic desirability features that would not be considered instrumental. Many of us just want to live in a society in which people treat us with respect. We value our own liberties and in fact we want to deal with people whom we can mutually anticipate will treat us that way. I mean we don't want to depend on the benevolence of other people. It seems to me I would hate to live in a world where one has to deal with a bureaucrat who has authority and therefore enjoys exercising his authority by making us be subservient. None of us like that. We prefer to deal with people with the morality of the marketplace.

Sinn: I'll take Peter Bernholz first on this moral issue, then Dalia Martin.

Bernholz: I am not sure whether the dividing line you ask for is so clear cut. You could argue, for instance, that if you want people to respect contracts as you respect them, this is a special case of the categorical imperative.

Dalia Marin, University of Munich: Let me turn away from the moral issues to a point that somehow has been neglected in the discussion. This is the connection between the international economy and the welfare state. For me as an international economist, the question is how can we sustain the welfare state and not whether we need the welfare state. We observe that countries that are more exposed to international trade tend to have larger welfare states. The reason is that freer trade gets political support because of a welfare state that compensates the losers from trade exposure. In a global economy, financing the welfare state becomes more difficult because it is more difficult to tax the mobile factor. At the same time, in the global economy the need for the welfare state becomes larger due to larger adjustment costs. How do we solve this puzzle? If we move in the direction of a smaller welfare state, then I think there will be less political support for open economies and that is something that we do not particularly want.

Musgrave: I agree with that sentiment. Globalization can be a menace as well as a blessing. It depends for whom. Tax competition interferes with the ability of individual countries to render social services, precisely at a time when labor in developed countries suffers from competition with low-wage countries. Capital, on the contrary, gains from seeking its most profitable location by moving there. But while distributive effects in developed countries tend to be unequalizing, labor in low-income countries gains, and inequality seen from a global perspective may be reduced. The Western egalitarian is left in somewhat of a dilemma, having to trade locally with global effects.

Buchanan: I want to make only one point. You have to make a clear distinction. First, there are policies that are aimed to compensate particular losers, as you move from a protectionist regime toward a free trade regime, policies that involve protection for those who are temporarily dislocated. You are sort of compensating them in a quasilegitimate way. That it seems to me is a warranted adjustment as you move toward globalization. I think you have to make a sharp distinction between that sort of transfer and the sort of generalized income redistribution type transfers. The latter is what Richard Musgrave has been talking about. As Peggy Musgrave in her intervention yesterday said, it is true that, as you move toward a global economy as the markets get integrated, it becomes more and more difficult to redistribute. If you have a competitive federalism or competitive group of nations in a genuine sense, it is going to be more difficult to carry out redistribution internally.

Niskanen: I have been trying to summarize the major differences in perspectives, but I feel less clear now than I did at the beginning of the week. The rhetoric that Musgrave and Buchanan use is quite different. In terms of what is behind the rhetoric, they describe normative situations. Musgrave tends to describe normative situations as outcomes that he likes, whereas James Buchanan tends to describe normative issues in terms of rules that he likes. The problem is that there is less difference there than I originally thought. There is a difference in the rhetoric, but I think not an awful lot of other difference. Musgrave says we ought to be willing to accept the rules of modern life because, by and large, it leads to outcomes that are liked. James Buchanan

says that he wants people to change the rules or revert to
rules of, say, pre–1914 because he doesn't like the outcomes
of the current rules. The nature of the argument is different
in each case but it seems to me as if there is a consequentialist dimension to both points of view. I would like both
James Buchanan and Richard Musgrave to elaborate on that.

Musgrave: I liked your statement. While I am a consequentialist, I also need rules to arrive at chosen consequences.
But what really matters are the consequences that we want
to reach. I am pleased to hear that Jim also cares for consequences. Concern with a constitution that sets basic rules then
becomes a pragmatic matter and not one of basic principles.
The more important question is, what are the consequences
that we should seek? Were it not for the troublesome trade-off
with efficiency, the consequences sought by the Samaritan
would be a fine goal, but I don't quite know what consequences James Buchanan wants, so I think that Hans-Werner
Sinn's question was very much to the point. But there is one
matter on which Jim and I agree. Our concern with economics should not be a technical matter only but should be seen
more broadly, including its relation to moral issues.

Buchanan: I agree with that point. The other day I said that
ultimately we must be, in a sense, a consequentialist. And
to be sure, I am partly a consequentialist, but I do think there
is a fundamental difference here. I was responding to a
comment earlier that it is hard to think of evaluating alternative sets of rules other than to include at least some
predictions about the patterns of consequences. But consequences in what sense? Consequences in a pattern sense are
different from consequences in a specific sense. My position
here in this context, and I do think it is fundamentally
different from Richard Musgrave's position, is a generalization of the market paradigm, the exchange paradigm, ap-

plied to politics. It is not consequentialist in the sense that there exists an ordering of social states or outcomes at all. What I am interested in is having a set of rules that would generate emergent outcomes from the interaction of people with certain characteristics of behavior in the institutions of this interaction. I don't need, and I object to, an ordering of the outcomes that emerge. What I am interested in is the way, the procedure, through which the outcomes emerge. Now if I start saying which procedures are best, then I get into predictions about patterns of outcomes to be sure. But if I observe someone with apples and somebody else with oranges, I don't want to try to say a particular allocation of oranges and apples in a final position is better than in the other allocation. If I observe them trading without defrauding each other, whatever emerges, emerges, and that is the way I define what is efficient. In that sense, I am not a consequentialist, so I do think there is a fundamental distinction here.

Sinn: What are you saying if one person has more apples and more oranges than the other?

Buchanan: It doesn't matter.

Niskanen: I think there is still some difference. I think Richard Musgrave would not accept all the outcomes of a fair game. I think you would not accept all of the outcomes of a fair game in the sense that you would judge the game by whether it leads to outcomes you like, whereas James seems to have preferences for certain kinds of games over other kinds of games and is prepared to accept a variety of outcomes, given values that are specific to the nature of the game.

Musgrave: Perhaps so, but let me add that Bill Niskanen's game analogy leaves me uneasy. I think that social life is not a game, and society's problems are not issues in gaming. Individuals may have different attitudes with which they approach particular issues. Their views of fairness may differ, and that means "right" has no unique definition. But reaching a consensus is not a matter of choosing what game to play, but of getting together on substantive ethical premises.

Niskanen: Typically the concept of fairness in that case is that you have agreed to the rules in the first place, and the social interaction proceeds according to the rules to which you have agreed. Now you seem to have an independent consequentialist argument that would lead you to reject some outcomes of that kind of interaction.

Musgrave: I would hope that culture and society will develop rules that generate what are worthy outcomes. I don't want to dictate what they are to be. As I said, Rawl's maximin principle is appealing, though perhaps somewhat extreme, and I am willing to include some allowance for entitlement to earnings as well. Each must determine what his or her input into the consensus-seeking is to be.

Sinn: Johann Brunner from Linz University is next.

Johann Brunner, Linz University: I would like to return to these two types of moral society introduced by Professor Buchanan. One is the moral community, and one is the moral order. The moral community is a type of society where people love each other and more or less live as if they belonged to one big family. Certainly, most of us would not like to live in such a society, probably because we would not like to depend on the love of the others as you said. But the question is whether the other type of society—namely, moral order, as you described it—is really the system we want to have. Of course, it is a necessary condition that one respects the other individuals. This is a condition for a market to work. But the main thing is that a community does more than only respect one another, because it provides some kind of assistance in case of risks or in case of being hit by some kind of catastrophe. One question is: how do we create institutions that help people in bad situations? This is what the welfare state does, and, in this respect, I think there is no alternative to having a welfare state. Of course, we have to make sure that it doesn't overexpand and that it doesn't create excessive claims on people. There is always a danger of that happening. But I don't think you can blame the welfare state or the public sector for ruining moral standards of the people. I think this is completely the wrong view. As Josef Falkinger just said: one main source of exhausting morals is the functioning of the market economy, namely, that private interests are rewarded. We have to try to create institutions against this problem.

Buchanan: There is much in what you say. I want to go back to the initial point about moral community, moral order, and moral anarchy. As I said, you can use those three stylized models to describe any society in terms of its mix among those three. There exist moral community within limits, moral order within limits, and moral anarchy within limits that describe behavior in all settings. In a moral order, you have people with mutual respect for each other in a generalized market. If society experiences a catastrophe, you get a shift very quickly as experience shows. When you have a catastrophe, people come together and form a moral community. Talking to people who lived through World War II in Britain, you find they all have a very nostalgic sense that back then was the only time that they were really a national community. The war itself brought on to Britain that sense of community. And so in a certain sense the subject of

natural catastrophes, wars and disasters, does in effect generate aspects of what you were referring to. You replace a
kind of moral order with a moral community. And so some
aspects and some of the origins of the welfare state can no
doubt be traced to that. I don't think anybody is suggesting
that the welfare state in its full sense is a negative value.
Surely, there are minimal welfare state objectives that almost
all of us would agree are appropriate functions for the state.
But what has happened, of course, is that the welfare state
has become overextended and it is simply not viable because
people are not willing to tax themselves to meet the claims
of the welfare state. Part of the problem is that it has extended into areas where the moral hazard problem has
become very significant. You have created classes of depend-
ents intergenerationally that you can't sustain. Whether or
not that has been a dominant force in the change in morality
that we have observed in this century, I don't really know.
I don't think I would ever argue that it has been necessarily
the dominant force. I always argue that it has been one force
and it is one that we could do something about. If you want
to come right down to it—and we were talking about this a
little bit in the break—it has been over a century since
Nietzsche said, "God is dead." The decline of the impact of
religion on morals in the Western societies is probably far
more important, ultimately, than the growth of the welfare
state. But also the breakdown of the family is very important. So all those things interact to result in the empirically
observed decline in moral standards.

Musgrave: Nietzsche, alas, not only declared the death of
God but rather enjoyed doing so, and the concept of community, as Jim Buchanan suggested, went with it. Perhaps
so. But community defined as total immersion of the individual in the "whole" is a dangerous concept, since it may

be built around diverse values, from appealing to abhorrent. Buchanan's third category of moral state is thus to be preferred, even though it remains morally barren. My own thought suggests a fourth model, where the individual not only accepts the tenets of the moral state but adds a sense of membership in and obligation to his/her community.

John Komlos, University of Munich: Coming toward the end of this conference, let me just express my appreciation for the great intellectual stimulation that we have enjoyed during the course of this week-long public-finance extravaganza. My point relates to a historical issue, namely, that it seems to me that in fact participants in an economy have often not accepted the outcomes in certain situations in which they were the losers. I am thinking of a situation like the French Revolution, the Russian Revolution or the Nazi takeover in Germany, for example, in which unemployment or poverty or hunger ultimately destabilized the political order. I think that the New Deal was also a response to a market outcome that people did not consider particularly desirable. My point is that the welfare state is, in a sense, a response to market outcomes that people didn't particularly like.

Sinn: Final comment—yes.

Musgrave: While listening to Jim's very interesting paper, I thought it might be useful at the end of this discussion— thought not to be taken too seriously—to reduce all this to terms which standard economists would understand. Though not an optimizing model, you have at least a diagrammatic presentation of what we are about.

The vertical axis records rely on a Hayekian self-interest-based social order, while the horizontal axis reflects mutual concern and a sense of community. The opportunity locus

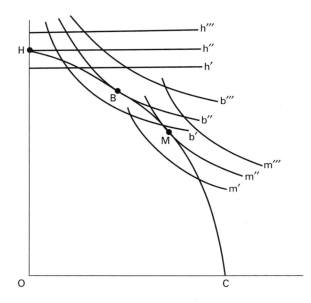

is given by HC. The three sets of indifference curves, *h*, *b*, and *m*, reflect the values postulated by von Hayek, Buchanan, and myself. Note that the *h* curves are straight lines while the others are sloped, with the *m* curves steeper than the *b* curves. *G*, *B*, and *M* show the optimal positions under the three preference patterns. Economic efficiency might then be added as a third dimension.

Buchanan: I think this is an interesting diagram, and I agree that in the context that Richard Musgrave has presented it, my position will be sort of between his position and Hayek's. My position would be a little bit up toward Hayek from where Musgrave might be. I think what is pervasive in a lot of the differences between us, and it has come out this week where we differ even more dramatically, is in drawing that frontier. I think, politically, there is a dramatic difference between the way we implicitly model what politics can do. Now you see, Richard Musgrave has no problem in just drawing this frontier because he is thinking of a kind of conceptualized idealized romantic image of politics, and this is where he would like to be. I would like to be just a little different if I took that romantic image of politics. But I have to be more realistic and look at the way politics functions. No doubt some such frontier exists, but I find it much more difficult to think that we can get very far out toward the right side of that diagram through ordinary politics. It seems to me that the majoritarian rent-seeking coalition building and any sort of democratic processes will not get you very far in that direction. Maybe the best you can do is somehow try to move toward the Hayek efficiency, but you are not going to even get there either. You're probably going to get somewhere else. So the real question is the underlying implicit political model from which each of us starts operating.

5.4   Summary

Hans-Werner Sinn

We have had a great week, starting on Monday with a presentation of the roots of the thinking of the speakers. It became clear that here are two different characters. James Buchanan represents a Southern heritage. He said that, as a southerner, he always had the feeling that he had lost the war and that this was important for the way he thought about the state, because the state was still more or less the enemy who had won the war. He had, therefore, developed an outlook that he characterized as antiestablishment, antistate, antigovernment, and, at one point, even libertarian socialist. By contrast, Richard Musgrave is the typical European intellectual, representing and going beyond the European public finance tradition as characterized by people like Wagner, Pfleiderer, or Sax. He is the thinker of social democracy as more or less realized in the western European countries, either in social democratic parties or in Christian democratic parties.

Our two scholars come together with Wicksell. They both think of Wicksell as their common ancestor, but they emphasize different aspects of his work. James Buchanan emphasizes politics as exchange—this idea that people come together from independent positions and do only what is mutually beneficial. Richard Musgrave, I think, puts more emphasis on Wicksell's treatment of public goods and his derivation of the result that public goods should be provided freely at a price of zero. So he developed his theory of public goods from Wicksell's thinking, and James Buchanan took the more positive view of it.

On Tuesday, we had Richard Musgrave's lecture on the fiscal role of the state, and he emphasized that we should not only take a negative view of this role. The state has had many great achievements. There are the basic functions of the state: the allocation, distribution, and stabilization functions, and he thinks that Wagner's law, that the government share goes up, not only indicates an aberration of history but is also a reaction to the objective needs that arose with increasing industrialization. The government basically provides the things that people want it to provide.

You have heard James Buchanan express a very different view. He argues that the size of the government has increased due to a common property effect. The tax base is considered the common property, and the particular expenditure that the government finances with taxes is an individual good that is consumed by particular groups so there is always a tendency to overexpand the government sector. Richard Musgrave has very strongly objected to this view. He does not believe that the government is a revenue-maximizing agent that simply has to be constrained in order to behave properly. James Buchanan, however, claims that, in fact, if you look at reality you see that some of these nice theories about the beneficial functions of the government do not have a good empirical basis. Public goods, for example, account for only 10 percent of GDP so the provision of public goods cannot really explain the size of the government sector we observe.

There was a major dispute about the notion of categorical equity and merit goods. Richard Musgrave said the state has a paternal function. He referred to the situation of children where the attitude of parents is definitely paternalistic toward their children, and he argued that society should sometimes also adopt this attitude. James Buchanan agreed that people may feel like that to some extent, but argued that there is no basic philosophical foundation for such government activities.

In his lecture on Wednesday on the type of constraints to be imposed on the public sector, James Buchanan argued the same way as the economist argues with regard to private market activities, namely, that it is the function of government to impose certain rules so that the invisible hand can operate properly and private agents can do the right thing. He wants to do the same thing on the higher level of the government: to find rules, constitutional rules, that induce the government to behave properly. But his answer is a negative one. He says it is not possible to find such rules. In particular, he criticizes the majority rule and shows that majority decision making leads to exploitation of minorities. Majorities always find it easy to take resources away from minorities. However, he admits that there is some normative basis even in the majority rule.

There was an exchange of arguments about the practical matter of what an optimal tax rate would look like. James Buchanan advocated the flat-rate tax because it would make it more difficult to make redistributive programs dependent on the deservedness of particular individuals. If there is redistribution, it should be a broad-based redistribution and deservedness is not something that the government should respect. Richard Musgrave said that a flat rate tax would necessarily require an exemption level, and this exemption level could become very expensive. He also argued that the flat rate would not redistribute enough and people at the upper end of the income scale would be treated too well.

We then came to the question of fiscal federalism where Richard Musgrave gave the basic lecture. He first talked about the functioning of the present federal system in the United States, the role of grants, and the role of different layers of government, arguing that each of them should perform the activity for which it is best suited.

The discussion then moved on to the controversial question of fiscal competition and we related that to Europe. Here the views of our two speakers were very different. Richard Musgrave argued that fiscal competition leads to an erosion of the tax base, in particular, that net taxes on capital can no longer be sustained. In fact he argued that capital would have to be subsidized in a situation of fiscal competition, and he called fiscal competition a glorious arrangement for rent seeking by capital. By contrast, James Buchanan argued that fiscal competition always leaves an exit option and ensures that no state can be grossly inefficient because, if it were grossly inefficient, the mobile factors of production would simply move away and that would discipline the state. He forecast that Europe would enter a period of competitive federalism rather than of strong centralization. Interestingly enough, he recommends that Europe should write its constitution so as to set out the rules of the game very clearly. He criticized the current state of affairs where decisions are taken on an ad hoc basis and the rules under which the different European states should interact are not really clear. I think this could be a positive message for policymakers that we can take from this conference—at least in this respect, they should go ahead.

Today's lecture I don't have to summarize. We have just had a wonderful discussion, a very deep discussion, about the philosophical and moral underpinnings of the ideas of these two prominent scholars. I must say that, in terms of lectures I have heard during my life, this was a real highlight, and I cannot expect to be able to attend a similar set of lectures again.

I am very happy that you all participated so actively. We had excellent comments from the floor, which is small wonder given the experts assembled here in this room. So let me thank you, too, very very much.

And finally, of course, nothing we do here could have been carried out without the help of those who did the administrative part, and here I want to mention in particular Alfons Weichenrieder and Holger Feist, who bore the major burden of making this possible. But I do not want to forget the secretaries Valerie Morfill and Gertraud Porak, and the students who helped here like Carola Rottmann and Alex Popfinger. And, of course, I am also grateful to the Bavarian Broadcasting Service, who will broadcast excerpts of this conference. The entire video recordings will be made available as a CES Internet Lecture.

References

Arrow, Kenneth. 1951. *Social Choice and Individual Values.* New York: Wiley.

Boadway, R., and R. Flatters. 1982. *Equalization in a Federal State: An Economic Analysis.* Ottawa: Economic Council of Canada.

Borcherding, T. 1977. "The Sources of Growth of Public Expenditures." In *Budgets and Bureaucrats, the Sources of Government Growth,* ed. T. Borcherding. Durham, N.C.: Duke University Press.

Brennan, G., and J. M. Buchanan. 1980. *The Power to Tax: Analytical Foundations of a Fiscal Constitution.* New York: Cambridge University Press.

———. 1985. *The Reason of Rules: Constitutional Political Economy.* Cambridge: Cambridge University Press.

Buchanan, J. M. 1949. "The Pure Theory of Public Finance: A Suggested Approach." *Journal of Political Economy* 57: 496–505.

———. 1950. "Federalism and Fiscal Equity." *American Economic Review* 40: 583–599; and "Comment on R. A. Musgrave."

———. 1954. "Social Choice, Democracy, and Free Markets." *Journal of Political Economy* 62: 114–123.

———. 1965. "An Economic Theory of Clubs." *Economica,* 1–14.

———. 1969. *Cost and Choice; An Inquiry in Economic Theory.* Chicago: Markham Publishing Co.

———. 1975a. *The Limits of Liberty: Between Anarchy and Leviathan.* Chicago: University of Chicago Press.

———. 1975b. "The Samaritan's Dilemma." In *Altruism, Morality and Economic Theory*, ed. E. Phelps. New York: Russell Sage Foundation.

———. 1978. "Markets, States, and the Extent of Morals." *American Economic Review* 68: 364–368.

———. 1981. "Moral Community, Moral Order, or Moral Anarchy." In *Liberty, Market and State: Political Economy in the 1980s*, 108–120. New York: New York University Press, 1986.

———. 1987. "Tax Reform as Political Choice." *Journal of Economic Perspectives* 1, no. 1 (Summer): 29–36.

———. 1992. *Better than Plowing: And Other Personal Essays*. Chicago: University of Chicago Press.

———. 1994. *Ethics and Economic Progress*. Norman: University of Oklahoma Press.

———. 1995. "Majoritarian Rent Seeking." Working paper, Center for Study of Public Choice, George Mason University, Fairfax, Virginia.

———. 1997. "Transcending Genetic Limits." Working paper, Center for Study of Public Choice, George Mason University, Fairfax, Virginia.

———. 1998. "Majoritarian Logic." Working paper, Center for Study of Public Choice, George Mason University, Fairfax, Virginia.

Buchanan, J. M., and R. D. Congleton. 1998. *Politics by Principle, Not Interest: Toward Nondiscriminatory Democracy*. Cambridge: Cambridge University Press.

Buchanan, J. M., and A. di Pierro. 1969. "Pragmatic Reform and Constitutional Revolution." *Ethics* 79: 95–104.

Buchanan, J. M., and G. Tullock. 1962. *The Calculus of Consent: Logical Foundations of Constitutional Democracy*. Ann Arbor: University of Michigan Press.

Buchanan, J. M., and R. E. Wagner. 1977. *Democracy in Deficit: The Political Legacy of Lord Keynes*. New York: Academic Press.

Buchanan, J. M., and Y. J. Yoon, eds. 1994. *The Return to Increasing Returns*. Ann Arbor: University of Michigan Press.

Clarke, E. H. 1977. "Some Aspects of the Demand Revealing Process." *Public Choice* 29: 37–49.

Coase, R. H. 1960. "The Problem of Social Cost." *Journal of Law and Economics* 3: 1–44.

Colm, G. 1927. *Volkswirtschaftliche Theorie der Staatsausgaben.* Tübingen: Mohr.

de Jasay, A. 1985. *The State.* Oxford: Basil Blackwell.

de Viti de Marco, A. 1936. *First Principles of Public Finance,* trans. E. P. Marget. London: Jonathan Cape.

Diamond, P., and J. Mirrlees. 1971. "Optimal Taxation and Public Production." *American Economic Review* 61: 8–27 and 261–278.

Elster, J. 1979. *Ulysses and the Sirens: Studies in Rationality and Irrationality.* New York: Cambridge University Press.

Fukuyama, F. 1992. *The End of History and the Last Man.* New York: The Free Press.

Gray, J. 1995. *Enlightenment's Wake: Politics and Culture at the Close of the Modern Age.* London and New York: Routledge.

Harsanyi, J. C. 1953. "Cardinal Utility in Welfare Economics and the Theory of Risk Taking." *Journal of Political Economy* 61: 434–435.

———. 1955. "Cardinal Welfare, Individualistic Ethics and Interpersonal Comparison of Utility." *Journal of Political Economy* 61: 309–321.

Hayek, F. A. 1960. *The Constitution of Liberty.* Chicago: Henry Regnery.

———. 1979. *Law, Legislation and Liberty.* Vol. 3, *The Political Order of a Free People.* Chicago: University of Chicago Press. (Reprinted by London: Routledge and Kegan Paul, 1982.)

Hume, D. [1739] 1911. *A Treatise on Human Nature,* ed. E. D. Lindsay. New York: Oxford University Press. (Reprinted by Oxford: Clarendon Press; New York: Oxford University Press, 1978.)

Knight, Frank H. 1933. *The Economic Organization.* University of Chicago Press, Chicago, Illinois. Mimeographed.

———. 1935. *The Ethics of Competition and Other Essays.* New York and London: Harper and Brothers.

Lindahl, E. 1919. *Die Gerechtigkeit der Besteuerung.* Lund: Gleerupska.

Locke, J. [1690] 1960. *Two Treatises on Government,* ed. P. Lasletter. London: Cambridge University Press.

Mill, J. S. [1848] 1985. *Principles of Political Economy,* Books IV and V. New York: Penguin Classics.

———. 1859. *On Liberty.* London: Thinkers Library. (Reprinted by London: Cambridge University Press, 1989.)

Mueller, D. C. 1989. *Public Choice II.* London: Cambridge University Press.

———. 1990. "James M. Buchanan: Economist cum Contractarian." In *The Public Choice Approach to Politics,* 403–430. Brookfield, Vt.: Ashgate.

Musgrave, P. 1991. "Fiscal Coordination and Competition in an International Setting." In *Retrospectives on Public Finance,* ed. L. Eden, 276–306. Durham: Duke University Press.

Musgrave, R. A. 1939. "Budgetary Balance and the Capital Budget." *American Economic Review* 29: 260–271.

———. 1959. *The Theory of Public Finance.* New York: McGraw Hill.

———. 1961. "Approaches to a Fiscal Theory of Political Federalism." In *Public Finances: Needs, Sources and Utilization,* National Bureau of Economic Research, 97–133. Princeton, N.J.: Princeton University Press.

———. 1981a. "Leviathan Cometh–Or Does He?" In *Tax and Expenditure Limitations,* ed. H. Ladd and N. Tidemann, 77–121. Washington, D.C.: Urban Institute Press.

———. 1981b. "A Reappraisal of Financing Social Security." In *Social Security Financing,* ed. F. Skidmore, 89–129. Cambridge: MIT Press.

———. 1981c. *Fiscal Functions: Order and Politics,* The Frank E. Seidman Distinguished Award in Political Economics. Memphis, Tenn.: F. K. Seidman Foundation.

———. 1987a. "A Brief History of Fiscal Doctrine." In *Handbook of Public Finance,* Vol. 1, ed. A. Auerbach and M. Feldstein, 1–59. Amsterdam: North Holland.

———. 1987b. "Merit Goods." In *The New Palgrave,* vol. 3, ed. J. Eatwell, M. Milgate, and P. Newman. 452. London: Macmillan.

———. 1997a. "Crossing Traditions." In *Zur deutschsprachigen wirtschaftswissenchaflichen Emigration nach 1933,* ed. H. Hageman, 63–81. Marburg: Metropolis Verlag.

———. 1997b. "Public Finance and Finanzwissenschaft: Traditions Compared." *Finanzarchiv* 53: 145–193.

Niskanen, W. 1971. *A reflection on Bureaucracy and Representative Government.* Chicago: Aldine.

Nozick, R. 1974. *Anarchy, State and Utopia.* New York: Basic Books.

Oates, W., and R. Schwab. 1991. "The Allocative and Distributive Implications of Local Fiscal Competition." In *Competition among State and Local Governments,* ed. D. Kenyon and J. Kincaid. Washington, D.C.: The Urban Institute.

Pigou, A. C. 1928. *A Study in Public Finance.* London: Macmillan.

Rawls, J. 1972. *A Theory of Justice.* Cambridge: Belknap Press of Harvard University Press.

————. 1993. *Political Liberalism.* New York: Columbia University Press.

Rubinfeld, D. 1987. "The Economics of the Local Public Sector." In *Handbook of Public Economics,* Vol. 1, ed. A. Auerbach and M. Feldstein, 626. Amsterdam: North Holland.

Samuelson, P. 1954. "The Pure Theory of Public Expenditures." *Review of Economics and Statistics* 36: 387–389.

Schanz, C. 1896. "Der Einkommensbegriff und die Einkommenssteuergesetze," *Finanzarchiv* 13: 1–87.

Schumpeter, J. A. 1942. *Capitalism, Socialism and Democracy.* New York: Harper.

Sidgwick, H. 1874. *The Methods of Ethics.* London: Macmillan. (Reprinted by Indianapolis: Hackett Publishing Co., 1981.)

Simons, H. 1950. *Federal Tax Reform.* Chicago: University of Chicago Press.

Sinn, H.-W. 1997. "The Selection Principle and Market Failure in Systems Competition." *Journal of Public Economics* 66: 247–274.

Smith, A. [1776] 1937. *An Inquiry into the Nature and Causes of the Wealth of Nations.* New York: The Modern Library.

Tiebout, C. 1956. "A Pure Theory of Local Government Expenditures." *Journal of Political Economy* 64: 416–424.

Tobin, J. 1970. "On Limiting the Domain of Inequality." *Journal of Law and Economics* 13: 263–277.

Tullock, G. 1959. "Some Problems of Majority Voting." *Journal of Political Economy* 67: 571–579.

Vickrey, W. 1945. "Measuring Marginal Utility by Reaction to Risk." *Econometrica* 13: 319–333.

Wagner, A. 1893. *Grundlegung der Politischen Oekonomie*, 3d ed., Erster Theil, Leipzig: Winter. *Grundlagen der Volkswirtschaft*, Zweiter Halbband, Buch 4–6, 893–908. Leipzig: Winter.

Wicksell, K. 1896. *Finanztheoretische Untersuchungen nebst Darstellung und Kritik des Steuerwesens Schwedens*. Jena: Fischer.

Index